ELIMINATE THE OBST
YOUR FINANCIAL, CA
AND FIND THE RES

## SURROUNDED BY
# *Champions*

## INSPIRATIONAL OVERCOMERS
## SHARE HOW THEY FOUND SUCCESS
## *...AND YOU CAN TOO*

# KAREN HUNSANGER

Hardcover ISBN: 978-1-7373917-2-2
Paperback ISBN: 978-1-7373917-1-5
eBook ISBN: 978-1-7373917-0-8

Cover and interior designs by Dino Marino

Edited by Terry Stafford

# DEDICATION

First, to my husband, who encouraged me to continue on my creative journey and patiently supported me while I followed my dream.

Ted Hunsanger

Second, to my two amazing coaches who challenged me to be my best, inspired my growth and self-discovery, and helped me find my voice.

Honorée Corder
Matthew Aitchison

# SPECIAL INVITATION

Would you like your story to be included in my next book? I am actively searching for the next group of Champions, and I would love to hear your story!

Visit www.KarenHunsanger.com to learn how to submit your information. While you are there, send me your email address to receive periodic updates and inspiration.

# FOREWORD

Every so often, a book crosses my path that feels like a long-lost friend. A book that shares and introduces (or reintroduces) me to concepts, ideas, and people I can relate to. One with a message that is a reminder that the most successful people have gotten where they are because they decided to be successful, looked fear in the face and kept going, and then went over, under, or around the challenges that popped up to confirm their resolve.

This book is just such a book. It contains the stories of people who are, beyond all doubt, extremely successful. You might have occasion to cross paths with them, and with a brief glance, see what they've accomplished. You may have concluded that they must have had a leg up, great connections, an easy path, wealthy parents—or all of the above!

The truth is quite the opposite; the ladies and gentlemen in this book have triumphed despite the odds, overcome challenge after challenge. They are people *who just don't give up.* Instead, they roll up their sleeves, double-check their attitude, and begin again as many times as needed to get where they want to go.

Every single person faces multiple obstacles in their lifetime, some more difficult or challenging than others. For example, a loved one's death, an unfavorable health diagnosis for themselves or their child, a devastating impairment caused by an accident, financial challenges, or even getting fired. These are just a few of the ones encountered by the inspiring individuals profiled in this book. These are challenges that could bring anyone to their knees, and no one would have found fault if they had quit, given up, or given in. What is remarkable about the people profiled here is that they looked each of their challenges in the eye and decided to triumph. They chose victory over victimhood, inspiring destiny instead of defeat.

Perhaps you can relate—you've found yourself (maybe more than once) in a puddle of snot and tears as you try to define your next move. You know you're not the only one who has come up against a challenge, and you wonder what others had done when they were in your shoes.

The book you hold in your hands is not just a collection of inspiring stories—it is a reference guide you can return to again and again when you need to gather your own inner strength to keep going. If they can do it, you can do it!

The first time I talked with Karen Hunsanger, a mutual friend had introduced us. I was struck by her quiet confidence and clear vision about the book she wanted to write, *this book*. She had a timeline in mind, one that meant she must delay *the project* she was excited to pursue. She was retiring, facing a move across the country, all while simultaneously building a new home. She had a vision and took each of these life events in stride, always remaining focused on her desire to write a book to inspire many. She was the perfect person to write this book because she, too, is the embodiment of the positive qualities and characteristics profiled by the individuals in this book.

This book is a gift you must give yourself or a friend who may be in the middle of a difficult challenge. I'm excited for you to read it and treasure it as I do.

**Honorée Corder**
Strategic Book Coach
Author, *You Must Write a Book*

# TABLE OF CONTENTS

# INTRODUCTION

## THE CHAMPIONS AROUND YOU

*"I'm investing in myself, I am investing in others,
and I am investing in my cause.
I know if I persist it will pay back in dividends
and it always does."*

**~ Simon Sinek**

Obstacles! Threatening you like a 300-pound defensive tackle attempting to keep you from getting the ball into the end zone. You've got to get past the big guy, though, because you still need to score points to win the game. Right?

So, what will your strategy be to break through and get over that goal line? What if you could find a team of winners to help you unleash your inner badass and beat your challenges like a Champion! How? I am glad you asked, and I will tell you.

In this book, I will share the inspirational stories of some amazing overcomers with follow-up and summary sections that will offer valuable guidance and resources. The format is easy to follow:

1. *The story:* You will likely relate to some of the stories as I tell of trials and ultimate successes.

2. *Your game plan:* Exercises and resources designed to help you define and defeat your own challenges.

3. *Winning points:* I will share what the champions told me are the detailed steps they took to overcome their obstacles so that you can learn from their experiences. We also look to other professionals for opinions and to offer additional helpful insights or resources.

4. *The Final Score:* Finally, we look at what the overcomers are doing now to further their careers and help others. If they offer courses or are coaches, speakers, or authors, I will tell you how to reach out to them and tap into their offerings.

Most of the people I am writing about, I am honored to say, I know personally. Though I am recently retired, over the years, I have performed in positions of employee and employer, entrepreneur, manager, corporate ladder-climber, and yes, once (a long time ago) as a rookie just starting out.

I have worked with, and for, many great people in the past forty years and have both failed and succeeded in too many roles to count. In all of those years, I can attribute some of my greatest accomplishments to my ability to both discover and be discovered by countless amazing Champions. They mentored me, challenged me, held me accountable, and befriended me. With them beside me, no test was too great, and no obstacle too tough to overcome. Later in my career, some sought my experience and counsel. To those, I was able to give back by teaching, mentoring, and passing the baton. Champions all!

A very good friend, who is also a young entrepreneur, tells me, *"I needed to level up my business if I wanted to reach the level of wealth I was seeking."* You can read about his huge success, how he beat his challenges, and how he went from investing in his own growth to leading others to do the same. You will learn a great deal from him and his story.

I listened to another friend and mentor as she described a horrific childhood. She had to overcome an unimaginable nightmare to create a normal life for herself and raise a healthy daughter of her own. In this book, you can read the inspirational story of how she broke free from her 'victim prison' and has gone on to help countless others.

These are just two of the Champions highlighted in these pages. Both share their resources and offer solutions to overcome challenges like the ones they faced. I promise, there are many more like them in the pages ahead.

The stories of some overcomers are not quite as intense but are critically important, nonetheless. What are your challenges? Is something holding you back from starting your own business? What if you lack the skills to land your dream job or climb the corporate ladder? Do you want to learn about financial freedom? Are you tolerating relationships that are holding you back? Is a serious illness or disability threatening your future? Have you been fired from your job? Maybe you have a challenging client, boss, or co-worker.

There are many obstacles to overcome in life, and these are just a few. It would be impossible to talk about them all in one book. But know this: most challenges are similar in that they can be overcome by finding the right help and resources—in other words, by recognizing the right Champions.

The bottom line is that you must invest in yourself and others to reach your goals. Beyond motivation, success is achieved through personal growth, relationships, and resources. Think about it. Why would you wait to find the true joy, happiness, and freedom you can have just by beating your challenges? Imagine having the help you need to get past whatever is holding you back from your dreams . . . to finally triumph over adversity.

You often don't need to look far to find a Champion who will take the time to mentor you or become the one you can mentor. Seek both with purpose, with tenacity. You can find some of them in these pages or be inspired to reach out and find your own. The Champions are all around you.

---

# FIRST QUARTER

## CHAMPIONS

*"Success is measured by the obstacles*
*which we have overcome to reach it."*

**~ Booker T. Washington**

FIRST QUARTER CHAMPION QUALITIES:

| | | |
|---|---|---|
| * Resourcefulness | * Courage | * Strength |
| * Growth | * Determination | * Commitment |
| * Goal Setting | * Forgiveness | * Giving Back |
| * Abundance Mindset | * Financial Freedom | * Strong Relationships |
| * Strategic Success | * Self Discipline | * Self-Healing |

# DIEGO CORZO

# CHAPTER ONE

---

# OVERCOMING OBSTACLES

*"The true test of a champion is not whether he can triumph, but whether he can overcome obstacles."*

**~ Garth Stein**

# DIEGO CORZO'S STORY
## INVESTOR, REALTOR, SPEAKER, AND COACH

The jet touched down with a sudden, fleeting jolt. As the wheels screeched on the runway and the howling engines were winding down, the Corzo family felt a heightened sense of anticipation and uncertainty. In that brief moment, the months of planning their move to the United States became a reality.

Diego Corzo was nine years old, and his brother, Gonzalo, was three, when the family of four left Peru for the last time. It was a send-off through tears and well wishes as they left behind the only life they'd ever known. In an amazing display of strength and courage, Diego's parents made the tough decision to move the family to safety and a better life. The reality was that the streets at home were desperate and dangerous. Diego's dad found it impossible to find work to support his family, and his mom was terrified after being robbed several times. But it was when the family's only car got stolen that they'd finally had enough. It was August of 1999 when the Corzo family landed in Miami to the welcome of Florida's sweltering heat and the promise of a better future.

Years after Diego arrived in the United States, the nation began to refer to him, and thousands like him, as Dreamers. But the truth is, the dreams he had for his future long preceded the title. Even though he was young, a fierce determination was already deep-rooted in his character. He knew the difficulties that came with this new start could never hold him back.

Diego deeply missed his family and the familiar surroundings of home. He had many memories of the happiness he'd experienced in their festive gatherings. He had loving thoughts of his grandparents. They were very close, and he knew they would miss him too.

Once the family was settled, Diego started school. He was grouped with strangers in a typical elementary school classroom.

The walls were adorned with the primitive artwork of the young students, and the teachers had kind faces. Despite the unfamiliarity, Diego found comfort among those children. They were just like him—all of them finding it hard to communicate with their peers outside of class because they didn't speak their language. He was grateful for the dedicated help of his excellent bilingual teachers, but it wasn't in his nature to be entirely dependent on them. Maybe he was as impatient as he was tenacious? He certainly didn't like the language barrier. Indeed, he was smart and driven. Regardless of the reason, he pushed himself harder than anyone else could have and learned to speak English, in good part on his own. By the time Diego entered the fifth grade, he was so fluent in English that he was able to attend regular classes. It had taken him only two years.

Years later, Diego started high school in a program for studies in advanced college-level courses. He already understood the importance of having big goals and surrounding himself with like-minded people at that point in his life. Plus, he was bright and determined and excelled at everything he tried. He wasn't satisfied with an average status and had such a massive thirst for knowledge that he continually pushed himself to reach higher levels of achievement. By that time, he had an impressive circle of friends that had become inseparable. As if their advanced studies weren't challenging enough, together they joined an afterschool club created to develop skills in science, technology, engineering, and mathematics. Diego was proud of their reputation. They were known as the "fantastic four." The team of overachievers won several awards in science and technology competitions. The real value of their education and skills would be well utilized in an extraordinary way later. Diego's hard work paid dividends as he finished third in his graduating class.

His accomplishments didn't come without significant challenges, though. All of his friends were driving. He excitedly went to the DMV to get his license too but was turned away because, as an undocumented immigrant, he would not be allowed to hold a driver's license. That was the first time in his life that he realized his journey would be different from his friends. However, he kept a positive attitude and laughed when he told his friends that he was lucky to be so popular with them that they would drive him anywhere he wanted. But there were times when he couldn't get a lift with a friend, so he hopped on his bicycle to get where he needed to go.

By the time he was ready to start college, Diego was so advanced that he would be allowed to enter as a junior. It was an exciting time, full of promise. Finishing third in his class was an impressive achievement recognized by offers of several scholarships. The excitement was short-lived, though, as he was hit by another blow. He discovered that he wasn't eligible to accept any of the scholarships. He was also ineligible for student loans or any financial aid. His immigration status created a seemingly impossible obstacle . . . again!

A familiar wave of disappointment came over him. He had no idea growing up that being undocumented would bring so many challenges and disappointments. But there was no time for feelings of *"woe is me,"* and that wasn't his style anyway. Determination set in yet again, and he was resolute in finding a solution. It was a fact that he would go to college, and emphatically, he declared to his parents, *"There is a way, and I will find it!"*

Diego had enough money to pay for one year of college. But he wasn't allowed to hold a job, so he worried about how he would ever pay for the remaining two years. That challenge was going to be tough to overcome. Still determined, he did what he always did and began searching for an answer. Multiple phone calls and blurry-eyed hours of research on his computer had passed. Exhaustion would not deter him, though. He had researched for what seemed like days. Then he found it! The answer was there, right in front of him. Was it possible? Even though it was not legal for him to hold a regular job as an illegal immigrant, it was perfectly legal for him to form an LLC. That was it! He'd found a way. He would start a company and as an IT contractor helping businesses create their websites. His training was going to pay off in a more significant way than he'd imagined. After all, he had won awards for his knowledge of technology, so he had the skills to make it happen. Starting a company was how he would pay his way through college.

Diego's first consulting lead came from a professor at the university. Diego had taken great care of his relationships there. Over the years, he'd found incredible support from the people he had come to know more like family than colleagues. The prospect sounded promising, and he was excited about the opportunity. He still couldn't drive, though, so he would need to hop on his bike to get to this first appointment.

The Florida air was thick with humidity in the early hours of the day in June. Diego's first website consulting appointment was vitally important to his plans. If he were going to pay for college, he would need to book many more of them. But at that point, he just needed to get through the first one.

Even before Diego jumped on his bike to make the trip, he was drenched in sweat. He prepared for it, though, and packed a towel along with his suit in his backpack. The plan was to make the trip in his gym clothes and then find a secluded place to change before meeting with his potential client.

Man, it was hot! But absolute grit and determination pushed Diego forward with every labored pedal of that bike. He was so focused on the path ahead of him that he was sure he could smell the scorching asphalt and actually see the heat hovering on its surface. He rode with resolute strength for the next thirty minutes. Exhaustion would not take its toll on him despite the punishment that was being thrust at him by the brutal heat.

As expected, when Diego arrived at his appointment, he was soaked. But he had plenty of time to slip unnoticed to the back of the building. Fortunately, the area was well hidden from the street. Propping his bike against the building, he proceeded to offload the contents of his backpack. He took the towel and dried off as thoroughly as he could before putting on his suit. Then he quickly ran a comb through his hair and grabbed his briefcase. After he tucked a few of his newly printed business cards in his shirt pocket, he casually made his way to the front of the building and into the business lobby.

It was a non-profit business, and the small entrance was modest but professional in appearance. There were a few simple pictures on the walls, and the space was sparingly furnished with a reception desk and a few chairs that lined the office perimeter. It was welcoming enough, but Diego still felt as nervous as a kid on the first day of school.

The owner welcomed him with an air of familiarity that put him instantly at ease. He was already aware of Diego's skills and knew about the awards he had won for his technical ability. The professor that recommended Diego had briefed the owner, who was impressed. So, the forty-five-minute exchange was both friendly and informal.

Diego easily secured the job to create the business website. It was an important first step, but he would need many more clients if he were going to meet his goal of paying his way through college. But he had reached a new level of confidence and knew he would succeed.

He was, in fact, very successful. Impressively, Diego went on to earn two degrees in college: the first in Information Technology, and the second in Management Information Systems. He paid for his education in full by building websites for non-profits and small businesses. In the end, he did it without incurring student debt.

# MENTORS, AND OVERCOMING FEAR

*"Being aware of your fear is smart.*
*Overcoming it is the mark of a successful person."*

**~ Seth Godin**

Diego had big plans for his future after college. He had a vision of financial freedom and wealth and felt sure that a real estate career could help him reach those goals. He didn't have experience and was aware that he wasn't surrounded by people he could learn from. He knew that he needed to begin to invest in himself.

He learned about real estate by listening to the podcasts of successful realtors and aggressively reading books written by real estate leaders and financial experts. He followed a talented realtor on Twitter and had listened to his podcasts, and one day they struck up a conversation and soon became friends. His new friend told him about the GoBundance Mastermind.

This group is self-described on their website as, "The tribe for healthy, wealthy, generous men who choose to lead epic lives." Co-founder, David Osborn, talks about the concept on the website video. *"No one succeeds alone. By having a group of like-minded individuals that will only stand for the best for themselves and their community of friends, we all achieve a higher level of living."*

Diego filled out an application and one of the other GoBundance founders quickly contacted him. He was overjoyed and excited when, one week later, he was invited to his first Gobundance event.

In August of 2014, Diego made the journey from the sultry heat of Miami to the cool mountain air of Steamboat Springs, Colorado, for his first GoBundance event. Once he arrived at the hotel, he met up with another young newbie. His name was Matt Aitchison, and the two became instant friends. They would remain friends from that day forward. (You can read Matt's story in Chapter 3.)

The two hoped they weren't getting in over their heads. They were about to be surrounded by a group of millionaires, and that reality began to sink in. *"What the hell are we even doing here?"* Diego questioned. *"Do we even belong here?"* Matt echoed. Of course, they were nervously kidding around.

The truth is, they wanted something more in their lives. They believed they could become wealthy and could learn how from others who were already where they wanted to be. They were going to engage with a new group of wealthy mentors, which would be their first step. They knew they were in the right place.

They were spending the night at a local hotel and would make their way to David Osborn's mansion the following day.

Bright and early the next morning, one of the group members came to pick them up. The Colorado air was brisk as they made their way out of the heart of town to journey up into the rural hills. The road was surrounded by soft green meadows sprinkled with the vibrant hues of hundreds of multi-colored wildflowers. The steep stretch of road headed straight up the mountainside and seemed to touch the clouds in the distance. With every mile they climbed, the mansions appeared to get larger.

There was an atmosphere of anticipation and excitement, and their hearts were racing as they approached the massive three-story mansion. The car pulled into a roundabout driveway and up to David Osborn's home. The beautiful rustic features were fitting for a home settled in the Colorado mountains.

They were in awe. Neither had ever seen a house so big. As they entered, Diego expected a level of grandiosity, but instead, sensed an unexpected hominess. It was welcoming and surprisingly ordinary with an 'everyday-people' feel to it. A light breeze flowed through the open windows and filled the house with the fresh outdoors.

Even so, when they crossed that threshold, they were nervous. Not knowing what to expect, they were a little intimidated and initially felt entirely out of place. But they were met with hugs and a warm welcome that set the tone for the entire weekend. The first hour was spent simply getting to know each other. But after the small talk died down, they headed outside for a game of ultimate Frisbee. The game—much like football except played with a Frisbee—was a great icebreaker.

The day wrapped up with everyone enjoying the amazing view from the Jacuzzi overlooking the city lights from above. Then they finalized the plans for the next day. The group was going on a hike to a famous destination known as the Devil's Causeway.

The following morning, the group gathered to make their way to the famous hiking destination.

The cool breeze was typical of an August day in the Rockies. Diego instinctively took in a deep breath as it brushed his face and was struck by the freshness of the Colorado air. He had been anxious to join this new group and was excited to find himself hiking with them at an altitude of over 10,000 feet. At that elevation, he was able to see far into the distance, and he paused for a moment to appreciate his surroundings. The rich blue skies hovered over miles of lush rolling hills marked by scattered patches of rock. He understood why hikers went there, as the beauty was astounding.

Suddenly, he became aware of a break in the trail just ahead of him. The steep cliffs in front of them were evidence that the group was approaching their destination.

The Devil's Causeway is a narrow, rugged, rocky terrain that interrupts an otherwise typical mountain hiking trail. Roughly fifty feet in length, it rests on top of steep sixty- to eighty-foot cliffs skirted by slopes that extend down another several hundred feet. The natural land bridge is a rocky path that narrows to as little as three feet in some areas. It is infamous for the thrill it provides some hikers or the terror experienced by others.

Diego knew that his new group of mentors were serious, self-proclaimed adventurists. However, that destination made it pretty clear that these guys were not kidding around. He was not as enthusiastic about this adventure as they were, though. He was deathly afraid of heights, and seeing the cliffs, even from a distance, made him extremely anxious. He had already decided to stay back and wait for the team to return. However, not everyone in the tribe was satisfied with Diego's decision.

Rock Thomas was not the only inspirational leader among this accomplished group, but he was the one who came forward. He began to challenge Diego on his decision to stay behind. *"Do you want to live an epic life or a fearful life?"* he questioned. *"You came here to learn to be like these guys. How will it impact your life to keep up with a bunch of badasses that you wish to be like?"*

Rock's words were powerful. Of course, he was right. Diego needed to remember why he had come to join this group. It definitely wasn't to sit on the sidelines. He had just started to form bonds with his new mentors, and he needed to show up. But he was terrified and continued to hesitate when Rock asked the final compelling question.

*"What will your life be like if you overcome this fear?"* That was it! There were many challenges that Diego had been able to overcome to that point in his life, and he would overcome that one too. He would cross. Though his determination kicked in, the terror remained. Still, he edged closer to the land bridge and whispered under his breath, *"What the heck am I doing here?"*

> *"The quality of a person's life is most often a direct reflection of the expectations of their peer group."*
>
> **~ Tony Robbins**

So, it began. There they were at the cliff's edge, and all eyes were locked on Diego. The entire team was watching and began to enthusiastically cheer him on. He slowly started to push forward, though the first step he took felt heavy and fraught with danger. *"You need to focus,"* Rock gently coached. *"Remember a time when you mastered something that was difficult. How did that feel?"*

Diego knew the feelings of pride and accomplishment that Rock was talking about. He'd experienced them many times before. *"I want you to think about what kind of person says yes to things outside of their comfort zone and breaks through,"* Rock continued, *"That person is a rock star! That person is you!"*

There were moments when the fear was overwhelming, almost debilitating, and Diego didn't think he could press on. But Rock redirected his mindset and continued to focus on him with firm but encouraging words. *"Diego,"* he said, *"I want you to think about someone you care about waiting for you and cheering you on from the finish. Make them proud."*

The words were profoundly heartfelt for Diego. He immediately thought of his grandfather back in Peru. He had not seen him for years, but they had been close, and he would be very proud of Diego right then. He could see him there waiting for him.

*"Don't think about what is behind you or below you. I want you only to see the finish,"* Rock said. Diego was terrified but kept on going. Every step was an unbelievable challenge. *"Just take one more step."* Rock knew that he needed to break down the overall goal to get him to the finish. He needed to get Diego to concentrate on taking one step at a time.

There were times when Diego was too frightened to walk upright but courageously kept pushing forward on his hands and knees. His innate determination, combined with Rock's words, and the value he placed on each of the individuals around him, would ultimately help him overcome the fear and get him through. He knew he would not have been able to cross on his own, and he was grateful.

His new tribe of mentors and friends, so supportive and encouraging, met him with cheers and high fives when he finally reached the finish. He immediately grasped Rock with a heartfelt hug to show his deep appreciation for how he had talked him through the challenge. The sense of accomplishment he felt was exhilarating, and his new group now felt a strong connection with him. He had earned their respect and admiration. Diego left that challenge with a greater feeling of power and belief in himself.

During the following six months, Diego went to six more events. In fact, he was invited to his second event while he was still at the first. David Osborn took an immediate liking to Diego and was so impressed by how he had shown up that first weekend that he asked him to fly on his private plane to another event. Diego had been bound by many restrictions because of his immigration status just months before. *I wasn't supposed to even be here*, he thought. *I went from riding my bike as an undocumented immigrant to flying in a plane full of millionaires. What are the odds for a dreamer like me?*

The GoBundance Mastermind group opened up opportunities for Diego to connect with more people like them. Those people became more than mentors. They also became his friends. He knew he could pick up the phone and call any one of them. Because they became so easily approachable, he says, *"I was able to learn at a faster rate than I could have on my own."* He was allowed the opportunity to leverage their experience and apply it in his own life. He learned about business and passive income much faster than he could have ever learned on his own. Diego recognized early in his life the importance of surrounding himself with people who could help him grow. That knowledge changed the trajectory of his life.

At a young age, Diego understood the importance of surrounding himself with the right people. He wanted to be around people who had a large vision of what they wanted to do in their lives. Most of the people he sought out were already doing what he wanted to do, and he was able to learn from them.

*"I realized that not only did I need to invest in my relationships, but I needed to invest in myself to be the person others would want to be around. But building a relationship with a mentor must be a win-win,"* Diego said.

Diego cautions about maintaining a grateful working relationship with your mentor. He says, *"In a relationship with a mentor, you can't always take. You also have to give back something of value. Always show gratitude and follow their direction, or they will not continue to help you."*

- **Other relationships**

Diego has always placed a high value on relationships. That is apparent in his story. He developed strong relationships in high school with his teachers and teammates and continued to build them with his professors in college. Those relationships opened many important doors for him.

*"I think that people often underestimate the power that relationships can bring because you never know what introduction might come from a relationship. Plus, you don't always know who's watching."* As a realtor, Diego says that 100% of his business comes from referrals. He no longer needs to market his business because of his relationships and reputation in his community. The secret, he says, is always to have something of value to offer to your relationships. Always be present and hear what the other person has to say.

- **Masterminds and Accountability Groups**

Diego joined the GoBundance Mastermind. You read about the value he received from that group. (The contact information for GoBundance is listed below). There are thousands of groups available. One place to search is www.meetup.com. There are many more websites to search. Also, search on social media platforms like Facebook, Twitter, or LinkedIn. You can also ask around. Chances are, you know someone who is already in a great mastermind or is part of an accountability group.

- **Education**

For Diego, getting a traditional college education was so important that he found a way to pay for it when it was seemingly impossible. He continued the technical training that he began in high school. That training was the springboard for him to launch his own business and land his first job. It was also invaluable as a means to negotiate with a potential mentor.

Of course, if a four-year college is not in the cards for you, you can also search out single classes, online classes, and seminars. The opportunities are endless.

## MORE ON CHAMPION RESOURCES:

In his book, *Own Your Career Own Your Life,* Andy Storch talks in detail about what he refers to as *"sharpening the saw."* He tells a story (similar to Stephen Covey's popular rendition in his book, *Habits of Highly Effective People*), about two lumberjacks in competition to see which could chop down the most trees and saw the most wood in a day. One of the two was shocked when the other beat him because his competitor had stopped so many times throughout the day. *"I was stopping to rest and sharpen my saw and was able to cut more wood as a result."* Andy emphasizes the lesson. *"You must sharpen your saw by learning (and resting too)."* He challenges his readers by asking what methods they will use to sharpen their saws. (Investing in yourself.) In his book, Andy recommends considering the following methods:

- Read blogs, articles, whitepapers, and books.

- Listen to audiobooks, podcasts, and audio classes.

- Take online courses or watch videos.

- Attend conferences, classes, and seminars.

- Get a formal education.

- Use social media as a learning tool, and follow experts, mentors, and masters in your field.

Andy Storch's entire book is packed with useful advice on how to invest in yourself for your career and your life. Pick up a copy and use the book as a resource to help you plan your career and take control of your future. You will get so much value from it!

## EXTRA POINTS:

- **Andy Storch,** Author, *Own Your Career Own Your Life*

  Andy is also a coach and speaker. To connect with him, reach out via his website: www.andystorch.com

Connecting with some of Diego's Champions:

- **David Osborn and GoBundance**

  *"The Tribe for healthy, wealthy, generous men who choose to lead epic lives."* (Taken from the website.)

  Read about the group, David Osborn, and the rest of its founders at www.gobundance.com. If you're interested in joining the group, you can fill out an application online. Watch the short intro video; it is fantastic.

  David Osborne is also the co-author of *Wealth Can't Wait*. Grab a copy on Amazon; it is a great read.

- **Rock Thomas**

  Rock is the founder of the MI Mastermind. *"We cultivate a community of high achievers who strive to create whole-life success and financial abundance together."* (Taken from the website.)

  To create "Your Game Plan" with Rocks' team, go to www.rockthomas.com.

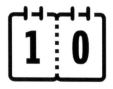

## FINAL SCORE:

On Diego's website, www.DiegoCorzo.com, he says, *"Your obstacle can be your biggest opportunity."*

Also on the website, you can find out about booking Diego to speak for your group, hiring him as a coach, or joining his House Hacking Club. Find out about the free guide and sign up for the course. Diego also has a Facebook Group, Rat Race to Financial Independence. You can find more information on his website.

Diego continues to work with other Dreamers to help them into their first homes by connecting them to DACA-friendly realtors and lenders throughout the country. The website is www.homefordreamers.com.

## FORWARD PASS:

*I started with Diego's story because even as he was faced with many obstacles, he remained positive and resourceful to successfully overcome every one of them. He is an inspiration and an example for anyone who is faced with a difficult challenge.*

*I followed with the next story about Honorée Corder because she possesses so many of the extraordinary qualities that are reflective of a true champion. Her story is one of survival, courage, and beating extraordinary odds to reach an amazing level of success. Now, she coaches and teaches others how to reach their full potential too.*

# HONORÉE CORDER

# CHAPTER TWO

---

# THE PROFILE
# OF A CHAMPION

*"Champions are made from something
they have deep inside of them;
a desire, a dream, a vision."*

**~ Mohandas Gandhi**

# HONORÉE CORDER'S STORY

## STRATEGIC BOOK COACH,
## AUTHOR OF *YOU MUST WRITE A BOOK*

As she ran, the force of every footfall shot agonizing pain through Honorée's broken body. Her blood-splattered sweater displayed the evidence of the brutality she'd just endured, and her vision became increasingly impaired by the swelling in her face and eyes. Her bruised arms and legs ached, making them feel unusually heavy, and her head throbbed. Yet, she pushed on with breathless urgency. How much time did she have? He would surely be close behind her.

Honorée was only eight years old when the beatings began. She'd often witnessed her dad unleash his anger on her mom in her early life. But then, a new era began. The terror was thrust upon her as a confused child, and in the years that followed, she was the main target of her dad's inexplicable rage. Her mom seemed to be content to no longer be the one in the line of fire. Maybe her mother was insecure from her contemptuous relationship with her own mother. Or perhaps she was angry because her mother had openly favored her brother. Whatever the reason, Honorée's mother turned her back on her daughter.

When Honorée was sixteen, her dad's cruelty sank to a horrific new low.

On that August afternoon, the fight was about money. *Her* money. The summer before her senior year in high school, Honorée had started working at her first job in a grocery store. She loved the work. It offered some semblance of normalcy and a brief escape from her otherwise harsh world. Honorée excelled at her job as a grocery bagger, and the success brought her a feeling of self-worth she had not experienced before.

Honorée was a hard worker and known for how she hustled to get her job done. She was also respectful, cheerful, and an avid follower of the rules. The combination made her highly desirable as an employee. The accolades did not carry over to her home life, however. Why didn't her dad appreciate the good girl that she was? She was confused. It also spurred determination and drove her to prove her worth to him.

In the family kitchen, Honorée proudly exhibited her very first paycheck. It was less than two hundred dollars, but it was a big deal to her! She knew it was just the start of a new chapter in her life. She had worked hard for that money and was proud of the accomplishment. Her dad was her only audience since her mom had taken her two brothers to the zoo. She wanted him to be proud of her. He wasn't overly impressed by her achievement, however. Instead of feeling pride for his daughter, he only saw a selfish opportunity.

Conveniently, that was the very moment he decided it was time for Honorée to begin paying for some of the family expenses. He reasoned that since her small check was not enough to pay her *"share,"* he would simply take the whole thing. *"Now sign it over to me,"* he demanded. *"No, I will not!"* she said defiantly. Years of abuse did not temper her natural desire to defend herself. Among her many traits, she was feisty. *"I'm just a kid; it's just not fair for you to take my money."*

Honorée saw his anger escalate in response to her disobedience. She had seen the start of these episodes before and tried to brace herself for what she instinctively knew would follow. Nothing could have prepared her for the power of his wrath that time, however. He had always been intense, but his eyes were piercing in a way she had not seen before.

She shuddered as she watched him furiously unhook his belt, knowing he intended to use it on her. There was no hesitation as he whipped it from the loops on his pants and began striking her with it, in between the forceful blows of his fists. She begged him to stop, but her screams did nothing to deter him. A neighbor, however, heard her cries from the other side of an open window and was horrified at the thought of what must be taking place.

The family living next door were strict Mormons. Shawn, a classmate of Honorée's, was one of the many children who lived there. The Mormon faith believes that anger is a weakness, and profanity is very offensive to God. The expression of either would be extraordinary.

When Shawn heard Honorée's screams, it shook him to his core. He had overheard her cries before and wondered then if her dad was crossing a line. But there was no question that time. He had never heard that level of terror in any of the previous episodes. That time was different.

Becoming enraged, Shawn ran to his neighbor's front door. He began to pound on it and shouted wildly at the thug on the other side. All who were within earshot would be able to hear him, but he didn't care. *"You are such a big man!"* he yelled. *"Come out and fucking pick on someone your own size!"* Shawn's behavior would normally have been considered reprehensible, but it saved Honorée's life that day. It was enough to distract her dad, who suddenly dropped the belt and rushed angrily toward the disturbance at the door.

Honorée did not hesitate when she saw the opportunity to escape the madness. She seized the moment, grabbed her purse and her check from the kitchen table, and bolted out the back door. Desperately, she ran through the yard, jumped the fence, and ran out into the street.

The Albuquerque suburb was the essence of middle America. The streets, neatly lined with stucco houses, were primarily occupied by average, middle-class families. Late afternoon was approaching, and soon those families would be preparing to sit down to dinner. Children were likely nearby, playing games, quarreling over the rules, and learning about compromise and other life lessons. These were the lives of ordinary families in the neighborhood. Honorée's normal meant focusing every day on survival, and many of her life lessons had been particularly hard and unfair.

The sleepy neighborhood did not reveal her secrets and offered no clues that anything was terribly out of place or unusual. Yet, physically and mentally broken, Honorée was running through those streets for her very life. The end of the summer was nearing, but the brutal heat still lingered. The air was heavy, and it lashed at Honorée's battered face as she ran. The stinging heat also made it difficult for her to catch her breath. Still, she needed to push on and keep running. Her friend, Merri, lived only about a mile away. It wasn't far, but she knew that she could be easily spotted on the street if he came after her. That fear kept her from looking back until she reached the walkway to Merri's house. Only then did she pause for a brief moment to make sure the coast was clear.

Out of breath, she desperately cried out and pounded on the door where Merri lived with her mom, Carole. Recognizing the cries of her friend, Merri rushed to the door and frantically pulled it open. When she saw Honorée, she put her hand over her mouth and gasped. In between labored breaths, Honorée started to explain what had happened. She didn't need to. Merri firmly grabbed hold of her and pulled her inside to safety.

The two of them had barely closed the door behind them when there came another loud knock. From the other side of the door, the police identified themselves with absolute authority. It was clear from their tenor that they were not there on a routine call. They meant business.

Honorée was stunned. So, her dad had not come for her after all. What a cunning move he'd made! He had a brilliant mind, but instead of using it for good, he used it to game the system at every opportunity. He had learned to manipulate the very structure that was put in place to help kids like her. Many of her teachers, friends, and anonymous callers, had contacted child services about the abuse over the years. She had spent time in foster care and had been questioned by counselors more times than she could count.

In the end, her dad was able to convince everyone that she was the problem. After receiving what was considered to be adequate counseling, she was returned home. She had no reason to believe things would be different that time.

It wasn't clear whether it was her dad or Shawn who called the police. But either scenario would not inhibit her dad's shrewd ability to manipulate the story. She knew that whatever he'd told them was sure to be a lie. She was only a kid. Of course, the police would take his word over hers. She hadn't considered that her injuries would have offered credence to her side of the story.

Honorée's heart raced. She quickly turned her focus on Merri to search for an answer. Carole was not home, so the girls were left on their own to grapple with what to do next.

Neither spoke a word, but Merri motioned Honorée into the bedroom. She quietly instructed her to hide in the storage space underneath the mattress of her waterbed. The wooden frame supporting the bed had drawers on either side. In the middle, between those drawers, was a small void that wasn't detectable from the outside. In it was a space just big enough to hide.

Once Honorée was safe, Merri opened the door. The police immediately got to the point, demanding that Merri turn Honorée over to them. They knew she was there! Honorée's dad told them that it was the only logical place for her to run to. So, they were confident that this was where they would find her. They informed Merri that Honorée had viciously attacked her dad and that she needed to answer some questions.

There it was. The lie! Unconcerned about the injuries he might have inflicted on his daughter, he brazenly made up a ridiculous story about how she'd attacked *him*. He'd likely thought about the possible ramifications of his actions, and in an attempt to save himself, he'd called the police. Then in a calculated move, he reported her as a vicious assailant. He was a coward.

Merri knew the truth. She also knew that the best way for her to protect her friend was to keep her hidden. They would figure out what to do later when her safety was secured. Merri countered the police and insisted that Honorée had not come there. Of course, the police didn't believe her. She was just a kid, and her mom wasn't home to verify that Honorée was not there. They were confident that they would find her in the house and insisted that they be allowed to search for themselves. So, doing her best to conceal the deception, Merri held her breath and motioned them in.

Honorée dared not move and barely took a breath for fear that she would make a noise and be discovered. She heard the search activity happening around her. At times, they were very close. The police searched the closet and behind the curtains in the room where she was hiding. Agonizing pain was surging through her body. She did her best to find some comfort by resting her head on the floor beneath her. Then, small tears began to blend with the bloodstains on her badly-beaten face. She did not feel the emotion that would usually accompany them, though. She was numb in disbelief.

The police search did not reveal the hiding place. Eventually, they declared that that Honorée was not there. *"We are sorry to have inconvenienced you. But if she comes here, call us right away."*

A short time later, Carole returned home to find the girls there. She cringed when she saw her daughter's friend. It was not the first time that she had witnessed the aftermath of one of these episodes. This one was ruthless, though, and it made her furious. Honorée explained that she already made plans to get safely to a friend's house and begged her not to turn her in. Carole knew that she needed to help her. She was not about to give her up.

# THE ESCAPE

*"It is worth remembering that the time of greatest gain*
*in terms of wisdom and inner strength*
*is often that of greatest difficulty."*

### ~ Dalai Lama

Honorée's family lived in her birth state of Ohio until she was thirteen years old. The family was forced to leave after her dad had alienated almost the entire town. The people there were aware of his years of abuse and knew him to be otherwise untrustworthy. There is no telling how many of them he had scammed, and she wasn't even sure he had kept up with the mortgage. She recalled that they had fled to New Mexico, almost in the dead of night.

Honorée's best friend, Heidi, still lived in Ohio. She desperately missed her and maintained contact with her through letters. Heidi had been her only trusted confidant and had offered a much-needed outlet for her to express her emotions. Writing the letters to Heidi was almost like writing in a diary about the continuing saga. She asked her friend never to mention the abuse when she wrote back, though. She feared that she would suffer repercussions if her father ever read those letters.

It was natural for Honorée to reach out to her trusted friend, and it seemed like her best option. She didn't have anywhere else to go. So, she called Heidi from Merri's to tell her what had happened. She bought a one-way plane ticket in a leap of faith and would fly to Ohio under an assumed name. In the 1980s, years before the 9/11 tragedy, it wasn't necessary to prove your identity. It was also still possible to meet your party at the gate of their arrival.

Honorée told Heidi when her flight would arrive. Then she cried as she beseeched her best friend to help her. *"Heidi, I am broken,"* she said. *"I am coming, and I hope you and your parents will pick me up at the airport.*" Heidi's assured her that she would be there with her parents to save her friend. The airport in Columbus was a two-hour drive from Heidi's home in Athens. Honorée knew that she was asking a lot.

Neither Merri nor Carole had clothes that would fit Honorée, and there was no time to replace what she had. The blood-stained clothes she was wearing would need washing so that she could wear them to travel. A jacket would hide her sweater, and a baseball cap would help conceal her face with the aid of some makeup. Reading a book on the plane would help her keep her head down and force her hair forward. She would stay quiet and to herself.

Early the following day, Merri and Carole drove Honorée to the airport. Honorée's stomach was in knots when they arrived. What if the police were there looking for her? What if she got caught? She hoped that her camouflage would be enough to get her through the gate and past any scrutiny.

Once there, she felt some relief. Typical of airport activity, people were too busy with their concerns to notice her. The airport staff was absorbed in moving the crowd successfully to their destinations. She was just one of the hundreds to them. So, she was able to mix into the frenzy without drawing attention to herself. Merri and Carole stayed with her until she reached her gate, and that created the facade of a typical family send-off.

When Honorée finally took her seat on the plane, she was able to relax a little. She'd made it! For the first time in hours, her mind calmed enough to allow reality to set in. She would not feel entirely settled, however, until she was safe in Ohio.

Honorée flinched when the wheels of the airplane abruptly hit the runway, but she finally felt safe on the ground. She followed the other passengers off the plane and began the walk down the corridor leading to the gate. Not having slept well the night before, she was feeling dazed, and the moment seemed surreal.

When she reached the gate, she paused for a moment to search the crowded area for Heidi. Then, she saw her. Their eyes met, and the two ran towards each other and collided into a tearful hug. Following a few steps behind, Heidi's mom caught up to the girls. She gasped in horror when she saw Honorée. Then she began to cry. *"What kind of monster could do such a thing?"* She knew that they needed to take the teenager to the hospital.

Honorée was a minor, so the hospital was legally bound to contact child services. In an ironic twist of fate, the Head of Family and Children Services had gone to school with Honorée's mother. The truth is that both of her parents were academically accomplished. Her dad had two master's degrees, and her mother had a Ph.D. in psychology, of all things. Honorée came by her intelligence quite naturally. The difference is that she was destined to use hers to help others and be the best person she could be.

It was remarkable that Honorée had no broken bones. But the bruises and swelling covering her body were heartbreaking to see. It was painfully evident that what she had endured was horrific and brutal. The head of child services was furious when he called Honorée's mom to give her an ultimatum.

*"I am going to bet that you don't want that rat bastard husband of yours to go to jail,"* he said forcefully. *"Heidi's family has agreed to let Honorée live with them. But you will need to send consent letters so that they can enroll her in school and seek medical care for her if she needs it."* He made it clear that he was in no mood to negotiate his terms when he continued. *"I will not press charges against your husband, but only if you agree."* Honorée knew that they were cutting a deal with the devil.

# A TIME TO HEAL

*I am not what happened to me.*
*I am what I choose to become.*

## ~ Carl Jung

During her first solo session, Teresa gave Honorée a workbook that would force her to go back in time and face her trauma head-on. The healing guide contained exercises that required her to answer probing questions about her feelings during the episodes with her dad. It meant reliving the events she had tried to bury deep into her mind. Despite her best efforts, however, the memories would surface and haunt her occasionally. Still, to share them, even if only in writing, would give them credence. The process was going to be extremely painful.

Teresa told her it should take five years to work through the entire healing process. *"Five years?"* Honorée scoffed at the prospect. *"I don't have five years. I have a year at the most."* The Navy would only pay to move her once after the divorce, and she couldn't accomplish that move while she was in therapy. More importantly, Lexi was only two years old. Honorée did not want to be in the middle of this process until her little girl was seven. She didn't think it would be fair to her. She needed to get through it faster.

Every Wednesday, the routine was the same. Honorée had a recurring business meeting at 7 a.m., but Lexi's daycare did not open until 7:30. Fortunately, her seventy-five-year-old neighbor, Betty, graciously offered to drop the child off at preschool every Wednesday morning. While Lexi was at daycare, Honorée went to therapy and then home to work on her written exercises.

Honorée spent the balance of her day at her computer working on getting through as many exercises as possible with few breaks. The process would emotionally break her many times throughout the day. She cried as she worked but bravely pushed on.

Honorée's close friend, Kristy, had a daughter in preschool with Lexi. Kristy picked up both of the little girls from daycare on Wednesdays, and Lexi became a part of her family for the evening. Once Kristy had the girls bathed, and in their pajamas, she called Honorée to pick Lexi up.

Honorée was exhausted and emotionally drained when she would get the call to pick up her daughter. After she got Lexi home, she read to her and put her to bed. Then she would end her day happy by watching some of her favorite comedy sitcoms. The following day, she would return to a regular work schedule, and she wanted that transition to happen without any emotional residual from the previous day. She became an expert at sequestering the process of her healing and therapy by limiting it to Wednesdays. She put so much hard work and dedicated focus into completing those painful exercises that she finished them in record time.

Teresa was astonished and told Honorée she'd never seen anyone work so hard. The five years it would normally have taken to complete the book of exercises took her only one year. Teresa said, *"In one year, you stopped the cycle. You will not pass the abusive behavior on to your daughter."* Finally finished, Honorée was free to move on with her life.

Shortly after completing her therapy, Honorée and Lexi moved to Las Vegas. She couldn't afford to continue to live in Hawaii on her own, so she took advantage of the one move that the Navy would pay for after her divorce. She had a strong business connection in Vegas, and it seemed like a great place to start a new life with her small daughter.

## FINDING A SOUL MATE

*"You can't do the right thing with the wrong person,*
*and you can't do the wrong thing with the right person.*

#### ~ Byron Corder

The mother-daughter duo had been living in Vegas for about four years when a friend of Honorée's told her she knew a great guy that she thought she should get to know. Not interested in the least about starting a new relationship, Honorée replied firmly, *"Um . . . No!"*

The same friend had been telling Byron similar things about Honorée, and he'd pretty much responded in the same way. *"I don't think so,"* he told her. He had gotten sucked into meeting that "perfect match" before only to have his expectations dashed. He would continue to put his effort into work and bypass the drama.

Completely undeterred and certain the two would be perfect for each other, their friend tricked them into meeting. She told each of them that the other really wanted to meet. *"You can't just hurt their feelings,"* she'd pleaded. Worn down by her persistent pestering, they finally agreed to meet, and Byron called Honorée to set up their first date.

Town Square was a new shopping center on the south end of the strip. There were various shops and eateries to visit, and it was the perfect place to walk, talk, and get to know each other. To their surprise, they spent the evening discovering that their friend had been right. They liked each other right away.

When Byron took Honorée home later that night, she felt a little apprehensive about getting too close too fast. When he leaned in for the kiss, she good-naturedly thwarted his attempt. She didn't want him to think she didn't like him, but at the same time, she didn't want him to have the wrong impression of her. They said their goodbyes on a light note, both of them knowing that there would be a second date.

Byron called again soon after. The conversation touched on the awkward goodbye from their previous date. *"What was up with that?"* Byron asked. Honorée mentioned her broken relationships of the past and how she had wanted to approach things differently, maybe try something new and with a bit more caution. *"You know, Honorée,"* he said reassuringly, *"you can't do the right thing with the wrong person, and you can't do the wrong thing with the right person."* It was so profound, and it is a quote that Honorée would remember and refer to often. He is genuinely a great guy, she thought.

Byron is the kind of guy who knows what he wants and confidently relies on his instincts. It is entirely possible that he knew he wanted to marry Honorée early on. He had even asked her what kind of ring she would like when it came time. She answered by telling him that she wanted it to be classic, elegant, and simple. *"Just like me,"* she joked. *"If there is any question on the perfect pick,"* she chuckled, *"just err on the side of 'Oh, my God!'"* They both laughed, and Byron decided that he would just have to know it when he saw it.

The official proposal was to take place at their favorite southern-style restaurant called Louis's. Even though she knew he would ask at some point in time, they ate there so often that she never suspected he would ask her on that night. He was nervously attending to the details and was late to a surprise party where they were meeting beforehand. Honorée was visibly annoyed. She remained that way, and they bickered at each other during the entire drive to dinner.

After the couple was seated at the restaurant, Byron looked at her and asked a simple question. *"How many people have you told we are getting married?"* Thinking he was annoyed at her and feeling unsure of his intentions, she just stared at him and tried to figure out how to answer. Not having her silence, he repeated himself. *"How many people?"* he insisted. *"How many people have you told we're getting married?"* This time Honorée wryly looked at him and answered his question. *"All of them,"* she said.

Byron chuckled at her wit and smiled a warm smile that quickly put her at ease. Then he pulled a box out of his pocket and held it out to her. The diamond shone like a star, capturing and reflecting the light surrounding it. *"Well then,"* he said gently, *"You're going to need one of these."* It was just like Byron to not get overly gushy at the moment. She knew how he felt, and of course, she couldn't be mad any longer. The moment almost took her breath away.

A mere eight months had passed since their first date. August 8, 2008 (08/08/08) had been determined to be lucky because it was a date that could occur only once in a lifetime. Its significance was not lost on the couple, and they joined thousands of others by choosing it for their wedding date.

The Las Vegas heat had been up into the triple digits during the day, but when the thirty guests gathered later in the afternoon, the temperature had dropped slightly.

The ceremony was going to take place on top of the covered Jacuzzi in the backyard. It was raised and served as a perfect platform, and the natural foliage surrounding it offered a lush backdrop.

The summer heat was relentless, but the ceremony wouldn't last long, and the setting was beautiful. The sun had just started its descent, leaving behind a romantic muted light. Lexi, then eight, was a cute flower girl. She stood close by when Byron and the minister took their places. This was it.

Byron watched in anticipation as Honorée made her way through the small gathering to meet him atop the makeshift platform.

The two shared some private moments true to the personal closeness of their relationship. But they held hands for all to see and touched hearts when they said their vows. The simple ceremony was softly lit by the last of the lingering sunlight. In the finale, when the daylight was turning to dusk, Byron Corder kissed his bride.

# SUCCESS AS AN AUTHOR

*"Sometimes, just being okay is a measure of success.*
*So is earning a living writing books and helping people."*

### ~ Honorée Corder

Honorée had been investing in herself and her growth years before she wrote her first book. One of the resources she used was seminars. She attended them to network and to expand her growth and knowledge.

At one of those seminars, Mark Victor Hansen (co-author of *Chicken Soup for the Soul*) told her, *"Everyone is a speaker and coach. If you want to stand out as an expert and grow your business, you need to write a book."* She was intrigued, but she wasn't a writer. How was she going to do that? She was a speaker, however. His advice was for her to take her best speech and craft it into a book.

Taking his advice, she wrote her first book, *Tall Order,* at the age of thirty-four. Initially, she wrote it to enhance and grow her business and share the seven success strategies she was teaching to coaching and business professionals. *(I will share these with you in the "Winning Points" section of this chapter—with her permission, of course.)* These were messages she was already talking about in her speaking engagements. Communicating them in writing allowed her to reach thousands of additional eager students.

As predicted, Honorée began to experience remarkable growth in her business. The more her name and her new book were recognized, the more her services were in demand. Soon, she was receiving more referrals for speaking and coaching. Best of all, she was able to charge more for those services.

Years later, and after she was married, Honorée began to reflect on where she had come from as a single mom. She felt motivated and knew she could help other single moms by writing a series based on her years of experience and the experiences of other single moms. She recognized the unique needs that these women have and published her series, *Successful Single Mom*. She helped thousands with her six-part publication. Of course, she didn't stop there.

Honorée continued to write, but she was also an avid reader, completing an average of three books a week. One of the many books she read happened to be *The Miracle Morning* by Hal Elrod. She was intrigued by the book, and it validated a morning routine she was already practicing. Hal Elrod's story captivated her. So, she took the time to write a great review voicing her appreciation and admiration for his work.

Hal Elrod read her review, looked her up, and soon recognized her as the published author of a successful series. He was interested in making *Miracle Morning* into a series, so he contacted her with a proposal to partner in writing it.

The rest, as they say, is history. The two became business partners and the co-creators of the hugely successful *Miracle Morning* series. Today, that series is translated into thirty languages.

## MENTORING & GIVING BACK

*"Leave everyone and everything better than you found them."*

~ **Honorée Corder,** *Stop Trying So F\*cking Hard*

As of this writing, Honorée has published more than fifty nonfiction titles. Her books are full of valuable business and life lessons and strategies.

Beyond her books' teachings, she educates others on how writing a book can enhance their businesses and their lives in her course *Publishing Ph.D.*, offered through her Indie Author University. The course highlights what she teaches in her book, *You Must Write a Book*.

Going a step further, she has created a mastermind, Empire Builders. She groups together authors and aspiring writers to help them (and encourages them to help each other) build related businesses and create additional income streams from their books. (See the "Final Score" section of this chapter for details on the course and mastermind.)

> *"I see people as better than they see themselves,*
> *hold that vision with and for them,*
> *and help them live into that vision*
> *until it becomes their reality."*
>
> **~ Honorée Corder,** *Tall Order*

Not all of Honorée s work involves writing and publishing. Much of her effort comes directly from her heart. Some of her most satisfying work has certainly taken her back to her roots.

In October of 2019, she became a board member of the Family and Children Services (FCS) in Nashville. It came about with a feel of divine guidance. Invited by a friend, Honorée attended a breakfast hosted by the organization. At the end of the event, she met some of the management team and expressed her desire to contribute somehow.

She told them, *"I really appreciate the work you are doing. I was a foster kid, and there were times when Family and Children's Service was helpful in my life. If there is ever anything I can do, I would love to help."*

It just so happened that one of the board members had to leave his post because of a family situation. She was asked if she would be interested in sitting on the board in his place? Coincidence?

She brings valuable experience to the board as the only sitting member to have ever been in foster care. She has a unique and compassionate perspective that can only come from firsthand experience.

Nashville has benefited in other ways from Honorée's residency there. FCS is not the only target of her compassionate work.

Because giving back is critical to her belief system, Honorée has been a Rotary member in almost every city she has lived in since she was twenty-three. She has always been drawn to community service and giving back and can do it in an environment that focuses on improving lives and creating a better world. The level of commitment she has always had to the organization would be commendable for anyone. But given her history of abuse, it is especially noteworthy. She could have just as easily been bitter and hateful. Instead, she is incredibly positive, kind, and giving.

## FORGIVENESS

*"I've learned to see the silver lining,*
*the blessings that come from every experience,*
*and to forgive and forget.*
*Having a selective memory,*
*one that allows me to remember the good*
*and release the not-so-good keeps me happy and sane."*

### ~ Honorée Corder

*"I have absolute gratitude and forgiveness for my parents,"* Honorée shared in the final moments of one of our conversations as she reflected on the reality of her relationship with her now-divorced parents. *"I also know that I am only human and can't have any*

*interaction with them."* She recalled the most recent contacts with them as being especially tough. *"I still want only the best for them."*

When Honorée spoke specifically about her mom's role in her life, it was with selfless emotion. *"I can only now think of my mom with gratitude and compassion because in looking back, she was doing the best she thought she could. She didn't know she could do better."*

Then all of a sudden, as Honorée often does, she lightened the mood and displayed her keen sense of humor.

*"Can you imagine if I had been born into wealth and privilege and never had a problem? I would be a freaking nightmare,"* she laughed. *"I wouldn't be on a mission to help and empower people because I wouldn't know what it is like to need that help."*

Her tone turned serious again, and she shared something she has often told Lexi. *"Being mad at someone is like drinking poison and expecting the other person to die, and that doesn't work."* Continuing, she added, *"So, the minute you can find the lesson and the blessing, or just forgive and release that person, that is a good place to get to. It's not that people will never hurt you or disappoint you or take advantage of you or abuse you. It's all about what you choose to do with it. Someday, I may write a book about it."*

I would read that book and take notes. But I think Honorée is already teaching us the lessons by example.

———————————

## YOUR GAME PLAN:

What obstacles are holding you back from achieving success? Plan your success strategy!

- Read Honorée's book, *Tall Order*, to tap into her seven success strategies. Follow her instructions to create a vision and list your goals.

- What does your self-talk sound like? Write out some positive affirmations, make them visible (for instance, on Post-It Notes on the bathroom mirror or another everyday space), and recite them daily.

- How will you execute your plan? For help on this, read Honorée's book, *Vision to Reality*, to learn more about her *Short-Term Massive Action (STMA)*.

- What new skills do you need to learn? Where will you get that instruction? Books, mentors, podcasts, coaches, masterminds, classes? You guessed it, research these and put together a plan.

- Are you giving back to others or your community? List the areas where you can add value to someone else.

**If you are struggling with an abuse issue, please reach out to a professional for help. You can check your local listings for the Child and Family Services in your area.**

(Read the "Winning Points" below, then re-visit this exercise for any additions that the review of that section may prompt.)

## WINNING POINTS:

As a matter of full disclosure, I will share that Honorée is my mentor and friend. I have taken her *Publishing Ph.D.* course (more than once) and am currently a member of her Empire Builders Mastermind. I am not unbiased! I consider her to be one of the most intellectual and exceptional individuals I have ever met. Both the course and the mastermind are incredible and life-changing.

When you talk to Honorée, take her courses, or read her books, there is a common personality trait that is continually evident. Her sense of humor is unparalleled. She often expresses that humor immediately following a serious sentiment or situation. It is delightful! When I asked her if she had three specific life lessons she wanted to share with you, the following was her response:

1. *"You are enough."* This is a sentiment that Honorée often expresses. She encourages people to stop doing what is expected by others and begin to do what makes their souls sing. A concept she discusses in-depth in her book: *Stop Trying So F\*cking Hard.*

2. *"You will be okay."* I believe she is speaking to all survivors and anyone who is working to heal or overcome.

3. *"Get a dog. Dogs are awesome!"* There it is, that humor. The more you read her books and get to know her, the more you will experience it. Thanks, Honorée! I have two dogs, and they *are* awesome.

The review of Honorée s life has been both personally profound and inspirational. There is a lot to unpack and learn from that incredible story. The winning points are countless and apply to both personal and professional issues. Honorée covers many of her life lessons in her books, so I often refer to them in this section. Let's go!

- **Surviving an unimaginable challenge**

Honorée had a support system of people throughout her life that she refers to as her "angels." Some were teachers, friends, parents, neighbors, and, of course, Family and Children's Services, to name a few. She is grateful for these individuals, and they were vital to her survival. But she also discovered that therapy would be necessary for her to heal.

As a young adult, Honorée went through therapy. In fact, as you will recall in her story, she worked hard on her recovery. It was a challenging and emotional time for her, but she recognized that it was critical for her future. If she were face-to-face with another survivor today, I think she would put her arm around them and tell them that there is no shame in seeking help and would encourage them to do just that. Remember her words of encouragement above. "You will be okay."

- **Relationships**

*"Be purposeful as you choose your inner circle of friends,*
*for your ten closest friends determine your destiny."*

### ~ Honorée Corder

Honorée feels strongly that the most significant measure of her success is credited to the relationships she has with her husband, daughter, and friends. Surrounding yourself with the right people, and developing strong relationships with them, will always have the most significant impact on your success and quality of life.

I have been asked why I included the wedding segment as part of Honorée's story and why it is significant. First of all, I love a happy ending to a harrowing story, and I thought you might too. More importantly, the lesson in that section is all about relationships and the difference they make in our lives. Honorée did not have a supportive relationship in her first marriage. She was smarter and much more selective the second time around. Her marriage to Byron has created joy in her life and helped increase her productivity and creativity in ways that would have taken her longer to achieve without having a supportive partner to share her life with.

### • Mindset and Affirmations

Honorée says, *"Having the right mindset can change your life."* She realized that, at one point in her life, she didn't have control over anything other than what she was thinking. Today she still relies on that concept in both personal and business situations. "Am I going to panic or persevere?" When things get crazy, she considers herself calm, centered, and peaceful, though she may have a mini breakdown of sorts once the storm passes.

Affirmations are one way that she controls her "self-talk." She writes extensively about this practice in *Tall Order*. *"Affirmations are vital ingredients in the recipe for success and personal well-being. After all, whether you think you can or can't, you're right,"* she says.

She explains that affirmations can be positive or negative and that they can work to your advantage or disadvantage. She says, *"They can be your strongest supporters or your greatest obstacles. The beauty of affirmations is that you control them once you are aware that you are already using them."*

### • Growth

Honorée's early career success relied extensively on her realization that she needed to learn new skills to grow into new job opportunities. Then her determination empowered her to self-teach many of those skills.

Learning—and the desire to learn—saved her. It certainly distracted her from the abuse of her father early on. But later, she continued to feed on knowledge to improve her life. Because she had not gone to college and didn't want to be financially disadvantaged (she detested the thought of being poor), she needed to acquire skills through learning and experience.

She didn't consider the lack of college to be a deal-breaker, however. Because she wasn't forced to learn subjects she was not interested in, she could focus on the things that would directly benefit her and help her reach her goals. She was influenced by reading encouraging the Bible and books like Napoleon Hill's *Acting in integrity*. Earlier in her life, a friend had given her Tony Robbins's book, *Awaken the Giant Within*, and it was a turning point in her life. It was then that she realized that she alone was responsible for her future.

Throughout her life, Honorée gained knowledge through several avenues, and she speaks about them often. Remember, your champions are not always people; sometimes, they are resources. She has relied on mentors, books and audiobooks, podcasts, masterminds, coaching, seminars, and more. You can too!

## • Success is a decision

*"A solid plan will cement the feeling in your heart
that anything is possible for you and keep
you moving in the direction your soul desires."*

**~ Honorée Corder,** *Tall Order*

Honorée knew that the odds were against her in terms of success. The statistics for victims of abuse and foster kids are not at all favorable. Remember, too, that she had a front-row seat when her father was living on the edge of deception, selfishness, and violence. Amazingly, she still chose the opposite for her life. It seems that her disdain for his deeds, combined with her unwillingness to accept the statistical expectations, may very well have driven her inner passion toward being the best person she could be and in doing good for others.

*"None of the people I went to high school with, and I mean none, would ever have voted me to be the most likely to succeed."* She laughs as she remembers her school days. She was intellectually gifted, but her grades were not good. Her home life did not offer a great study atmosphere, so she barely got by.

She could have chosen a darker life, perhaps by becoming a drug dealer or a drug addict. Honestly, the idea of ever going to jail was terrifying to her. She says, *"If I have an addiction, it is to success and being a better person."* She continues by revealing where her heart is in terms of surviving and her success. *"Sometimes, just being okay is a measure of success. But the fact that I am still here, I survived, and have never been in jail is evidence that I beat the odds."*

### • Giving back

I know few individuals, if any, who are more charitable with their time and money than Honorée is. One reason is that she feels herself to be one of the lucky ones to have received the kindness of others when she needed it most in her life.

When listening to her, you can tell she also considers giving back a duty and something for which she is divinely guided. She is certain that if that hadn't been the case, she wouldn't have survived. She does it for an important reason. Her gifts are in the wisdom of her written messages and in her contributions to her community.

## SEVEN SUCCESS STRATEGIES

In *Tall Order*, Honorée shares seven success strategies. *(As promised, I am sharing these with Honorée's permission. Please note that I am only touching briefly on her strategy. You will need to pick up a copy of the book to read the details. You will be so happy you did.)*

Let's take a peek at her "Master Strategies."

1. **Create Your Vision:** Identify your desired direction and purpose. Take the time to be clear about your future and picture new possibilities.

2. **Visible Goals:** Set your goals based on what you identified as the direction of your future. Be specific about your goals and write them down.

3. **The 100-Day Rule:** Whatever you are doing right now will affect your life and business in 100 days.

4. **Find a Masterful Mentor:** Honorée writes, *"An ideal mentor is someone who has started a business in your industry, been successful both personally and professionally, and who has probably made many of the mistakes you hope to avoid."*

5. **Use Time-Multiplier Strategies:** Start an hour earlier in the morning and spend one hour a week planning the week ahead.

6. **The Power of Association:** Honorée writes, *"Whom you associate with, and whom you have in your intimate and inner circles, can make or break you."*

7. **Unlock Your Super Alter Ego with a Coach:** One of Honorée's coaches helped her increase her productivity and income by 300% in ninety days. She gained insights into how she was utilizing her time, identifying bigger goals, defining a larger vision, and accountability.

# STMA: *SHORT TERM MASSIVE ACTION*

*"Anything is possible when you believe you can,
have a plan, and take consistent, persistent,
and intentional action towards its attainment."*

~ **Honorée Corder,** *Vision to Reality*

Early in her life, Honorée didn't have strong personal relationships to support her dreams. But she knew what she wanted and developed the habit of writing goals and plans for her future on her own. In her twenties, she learned that writing them down and visualizing them daily helped her focus on them. Remember how her first husband offered her zero support and even belittled her? (Don't I wish I had been so savvy in my twenties, or thirties, for that matter!) The good news is that you can learn new habits no matter your starting point.

During the years that followed, Honorée took action to execute her plans. After all, a written plan is just an essay unless you take action to implement it. Right? It might have some entertainment value, but it will not move you forward toward your goals.

Honorée calls the action plan she developed *Short Term Massive Action* or *STMA*. She teaches the system in her book, *Vision to Reality*. Perhaps one of the most impressive things about the system is that Honorée developed it solely for her own use years before she'd even considered coaching and training. It came from her personal experiences.

One of the main topics she teaches in her book pertains to mindset and how critical it is to maintain a positive can-do attitude to achieve your goals. In other words, believe in yourself!

It took Honorée years to develop *STMA* by studying successful people, reading hundreds of books, attending seminars, and finally, a lot of practice. You can take a more straightforward, less time-consuming route, and simply pick up her book *Vision to Reality*, where you can learn how to implement her fantastic system in your life. Lucky you!

## FINAL SCORE:

Everything Honorée can be found on her website: www.HonoreeCorder.com.

You might want to work with her if:

1. You want to write a book but don't know where to start.

2. You have an unpublished book, and you're not sure what needs to be done or how to do it.

3. Your book is almost ready to launch.

4. You have a book, yet it's underperforming.

5. You want to turn your expertise into a million-dollar brand, with multiple streams of income, utilizing, in part, your book.

For information on the *Publishing Ph.D.* course, *Empire Builders Mastermind, Building a Million Dollar Book Business,* and *The Collective Mastermind,* visit Honorée's website, listed above.

NOTE: Honorée began to experience remarkable growth in her business after she wrote her first book. This is what she teaches in her online course *Publishing Ph.D.*

You can also book Honorée for Speaking Engagements or email her at Assisitant@HonoreeCorder.com for more details or questions.

Of course, all of Honorée's publications can be found on Amazon.com.

## FORWARD PASS:

*In the next section, you will read the stories of two accomplished leaders and about the importance of relationships in achieving success.*

*Matt Aitchison's story is about a young leader's discovery of how critical it is to develop quality relationships. He learned to surround himself with people who have the values and knowledge he wanted to emulate.*

*Mike Carney's story is one of a seasoned leader that delivers an important message about how to treat people with deference. His wisdom is extraordinary and inspiring.*

# SECOND QUARTER

## RELATIONSHIPS & LEADERSHIP

*"Relationships are the foundation of Leadership."*

**~ John C. Maxwell**

SECOND QUARTER CHAMPION QUALITIES:

* Integrity

* Character

* Selflessness

* Growth

* Tenacity

* Investing in Others

* Selective of Friends and Colleagues

* Accountability

* Kindness (The Golden Rule)

# MATT AITCHISON

# CHAPTER THREE

# THE POWER OF RELATIONSHIPS

*"Anything is possible when you have the right people there to support you."*

**~ Misty Copeland**

# MATT AITCHISON'S STORY
## CEO AND PRESIDENT OF
## VAULT INVESTMENT PROPERTIES,
## FOUNDER OF RICH LIFE ACADEMY

Outside of the hospital, the fall air was crisp, and the fallen leaves were dancing across the earth's surface to the song of a soft breeze. Inside, however, the peace and comfort of that setting went unnoticed. Matt's stepmom, Julie, was sick, and inside her hospital room, the air was only filled with uncertainty and concern.

Matt's parents, Mike and Sonya, divorced when he was only three years old, and Mike married Julie when Matt was only five. He was too young to remember that she hadn't always been there. In his earliest memories of her, she touched his life immensely, and over the following years, their bond grew strong. She was his second mom, and he treasured their relationship.

Mike, Julie, and Sonya remained friends throughout Matt's childhood. These rare and selfless friendships created a partnership in his upbringing that brought immeasurable stability and support into his life. Taking turns between the two households became a normal way of life for Matt. Each of them felt as much like home as the other.

Matt was a sixteen-year-old sophomore in high school when he received word from his mom that Julie was seriously ill and in the hospital. His head was spinning with the news when Sonya picked him up at school. The car ride to the hospital was quiet, but his mind raced with questions that couldn't be answered yet.

When Matt entered the hospital room, he could sense the seriousness of Julie's condition. She had a frailness about her that was foreign to him. She was only forty years old and had always seemed so strong. But within a matter of hours after arriving at the hospital, she was diagnosed with a rare form of leukemia.

Over the next six days, Matt and his dad stayed at Julie's side. Sonya brought him supplies from home so that he could keep vigil. But the wait was of no avail, as with every passing day, Julie's condition only became worse. Within days, the cruel and sudden illness took her life.

# FRIENDS, FAMILY, AND GROWING THROUGH MISTAKES

*"It's almost impossible to live the right life when you have the wrong friends."*

### ~ Craig Groeschel

Matt had never experienced the pain of losing someone close to him, and Julie's passing left him feeling deeply hurt and angry. Her sudden death made him question his spirituality and the fairness of life. He wondered how something so bad could happen to someone so good, and if there was any reward for living a good life.

Matt's attitude toward life changed. Behind the scenes, he became a rebellious teenager. His mom and dad didn't suspect anything because he was normal and respectful at home. But once he was outside of the house, Matt surrounded himself with an unruly group of friends. He filled his weekends with a combination of raucous parties and questionable choices.

Just as he had done before Julie's death, Matt spent many of his after-school hours at basketball practice. It offered a welcome escape from the pain of his family's loss. He loved the game's challenge and welcomed the break so that he could focus solely on improving his skill.

At one of those basketball practices early in his senior year, a known troublemaker and rival to his circle of friends began taunting the players through the large windows of the gym. The team laughed at him and shot back with jeers and hecklings of their own, but it became clear that their adversary was getting more and more agitated.

The guy waited for them outside and, for some unknown reason, singled Matt out. Matt was not about to back down in front of his teammates, and a fight broke out. Unfortunately, the school had a zero-tolerance policy towards fighting, and that fight got him expelled.

All of a sudden, the behavior Matt had been so successful at keeping hidden was exposed. He felt horrible at the thought of disappointing his parents. He was one of the lucky kids that could always count on his parents' strong support. Not everyone in his circle of friends had that positive home environment.

Matt was embarrassed and ashamed. That was not the person he was deep inside, and he knew that he needed to make things right. It would be a tough road to get back in school, but he didn't care what it took.

Not only did he need to ditch his circle of friends, but to get back into school, he had to face some stringent requirements. He would need to get exceptional grades at a continuing education school and complete several hours of community service.

Matt was determined to get back into school and pushed himself hard. He worked tirelessly through many long and grueling hours. He was successful at overcoming his setback, though, and in the end, he got back to school in time to graduate with his class. He had worked so hard that the expulsion was expunged from his record, and he was accepted to attend U.C. Santa Barbara. Not only had he accomplished a seemingly-impossible feat, but he was also going on to college. With his family's support and his natural drive and resolve, he had turned a hard lesson into a huge win.

# A NEW START AND SECOND CHANCES

*"Experience is a hard teacher because
she gives us the test first and the lesson afterward."*

**~ Vernon Law**

With his high school days and old friends behind him, Matt moved from home to go to school in Santa Barbara. He was excited for a fresh beginning in the quaint beach city.

His first year in college was relatively uneventful. He spent most of his time making new friends and becoming familiar with his environment. In his second year, however, he became a little too comfortable in his new setting. He seemed to forget his previous life lessons and started to slip back into some of his old weekend habits. He was not surrounding himself with quality friends.

One Saturday night, he and a group of those friends went to a party and began drinking. It had become a typical weekend scene for this group of college kids. But on that night, Matt drank way too much alcohol way too fast. The night that had started out full of laughs and crazy antics soon became a drunken blur that Matt would have a hard time remembering later. It was well into the hours of the following morning before he could piece together any of the night's events.

Matt struggled to open his eyes through the fierce throbbing pain in his head. He grimaced as the sickening smell of vomit abruptly blasted his senses and caused a burning queasiness in the pit of his stomach. "Where the hell am I?" he questioned as he began to lift his head and slowly survey his surroundings. He was groggy but awake and horrified when he suddenly realized he was in a jail holding cell surrounded by some of the most frightening people he had ever seen.

Slowly, some of the details of the night began to come back to him, and the reality of what he had done started to sink in. He had a vague memory of a party getting out of control. "Damn it!" He had gotten into another fight and punched a guy in the face. That time, he was sitting in jail and knew he must be in some deep shit.

Shortly after his arrest, Matt became aware of the severity of what he had done and the penalty he could face. The district attorney wanted to charge him with felony assault and battery. It was a charge that carried with it the possibility of two years in jail. Honestly, the thought of returning to jail scared the heck out of him. What would his future look like? The uncertainty was agonizing. His life was on hold through months of uncomfortable depositions and tough legal discussions.

Matt had made a terrible mistake that left him feeling like a failure. He was pretty tough on himself, knowing that he was better than that. He had not been living up to his full potential. But he couldn't allow his mistake to define his future. He needed to forgive himself and make it through that life lesson.

Matt began to come to terms with his situation and realized that he needed to work through the process and make things right by doing whatever it would take to pay his debt. He reached out to apologize to the other guy in the fight. Thankfully, that guy was okay, and Matt was extremely thankful.

He was still nervous about the price he would be required to pay for his mistake. Would he be forced to quit school? He needed to prepare for the worst and put a plan together for his future beyond this episode in his life, but he was ready to accept his fate.

Then, just as he had resolved to accept the decision, regardless of what came down, the truly unexpected happened. In a call with his attorney, Matt found out that the other guy in the fight didn't want any additional attention drawn to it and didn't want to press charges. The DA then determined he lacked the evidence to prosecute Matt and didn't have a case. And just like that, the charges were dropped. Matt was stunned!

It was a fantastic turn of events, a true gift, as he had been given another chance. He wasn't going to let it go to waste. It was time to start putting his life back together.

Matt started to make changes in his life, beginning with looking hard at the individuals he had been spending most of his time with. Walking away from people in his circle of friends would be difficult. But if he was going to avoid repeating his mistakes and begin to steer his life in the right direction, he needed to purge his toxic relationships.

## MENTORS AND THE FIRST FLIP

*"Having mentors shortened my learning curve
and accelerated my success. They helped me to steer clear of
mistakes, tap into resources, and build relationships
that would have taken me decades to develop on my own."*

### ~ Matt Aitchison

When Matt was still in college, he was introduced to business while at his first job working for a local entrepreneur. He didn't understand what it meant to have a mentor at the time but later realized that this boss had been his first. He taught Matt about the responsibilities and activities that go along with being a business owner. Along the way, Matt was introduced to his boss's lifestyle as an entrepreneur. It was a lavish lifestyle, and he wanted to model it in his own life. Actually, he wanted to make enough money to surpass that lifestyle someday.

Matt left that job and moved back home after he finished school. Once there, it was time to figure out how to earn an income. He'd learned a little about real estate earlier in his life. As a kid, he'd attended several real estate seminars with his mom, Sonya. The events inspired him, and he was intrigued by the amount of wealth that seemed possible from investing in real estate. Listening to the speakers captivated him. Perhaps he'd had a vision when he accurately predicted, *"Someday that will be me on that stage."* He decided that real estate as a career choice could lead him to the lifestyle and amount of money he wanted to make.

Matt knew that if he was going to turn real estate investing into something that he could leverage for the rest of his life, he needed to learn, gain experience, and develop resources and connections. He hadn't surrounded himself with the right people before, but he would now. Matt needed to be having conversations with experienced people who had the level of success he wanted to achieve. He needed a mentor.

When he began his search, he found a local house flipper who was interested in him. Matt readily agreed to work for him for free in exchange for the training and experience he sought.

Several months had gone by when Matt began to realize that he was working for a shady guy. He'd witnessed him cutting corners and covering things up. To make matters worse, Matt was doing all of the work, and this dishonest flipper was raking in a bunch of cash. After ten months of working for free, reality set in. *I know how to do this!* Matt thought. *Why am I making this guy so much money instead of working for myself?* Furthermore, he didn't want to risk having a bad reputation follow him to his future business. There were rewards to be gained in the experience, though. In ten months, he had expanded his knowledge and acquired a new level of confidence. He took those lessons along with his integrity when he walked away from that job.

He'd been working for free. So, he was broke, loaded with credit card debt, and still living at home. It was laughable to think he could get a loan, and he certainly couldn't qualify for a mortgage. Even so, he knew that if he could find a deal, he could secure the money to make it happen.

Matt was more determined than ever to gain experience and learn. He began to read more books, listen to podcasts, and attend conferences and seminars to make connections. Knowing that he needed to invest in himself and surround himself with the right people, he joined the GoBundance Mastermind. That group of wealthy mentors would teach him about creating good habits with money, health, and relationships.

It was also time to seek out a great real estate mentor. He'd learned from his first mistake, so he asked himself some key questions. *Who has the reputation, experience level, and business model that I can best learn from? Do they have the lifestyle, family, and core values I am seeking?* He wasn't merely looking for a mentor for the sake of having one. He wanted to find one he could align with.

Being selective about a new mentor paid off. Matt finally found a real estate champion. He began wholesaling their properties and learning how they were managing their business. It wasn't long before he was inspired to go out on his own. It wouldn't be easy, however. He started by sending out some simple direct mail pieces and walking for endless hours door-knocking. Then he began getting up at three every morning to go out into the dark to put up bandit signs to advertise his services. *I might avoid the 'sign police' if I go out early in the morning,* he thought as he laughed to himself. He was working hard and trying different things to see what would find him his first flip.

After numerous calls from angry people telling him to "eff off" and ordering him to remove his ugly signs from their neighborhoods, he got *the* call he had been waiting for. He humbly thought that he'd gotten lucky, but truthfully, his consistency, tenacity, and hard work were about to pay off. Matt arranged to meet his first potential client at the home of that client's elderly mother.

*Imagine that a smell could punch you in the face. This one does! This is the foulest cat smell I have ever experienced,* Matt thought when walking into his first flip as a new investor. The call had come from an anxious son who traveled to Sacramento from out of state. His mother was having severe health and financial issues. He needed to relocate her and sell her home as quickly as possible. The son was desperate for help and asked Matt to look at the rundown house to see if it had any remaining value. Could it even be salvaged? He had tried to warn Matt about what was to come. *"Prepare yourself for the worst,"* he cautioned. *"The place is in pretty rough shape."*

Finally, after months of preparing for the moment, Matt walked through the door of his first flip. The son had told him that his mother was a cat fanatic. But as Matt entered, it became immediately evident that she was also a hoarder. There was so much trash on the floor that stepping over it was not an option. With every step he took, he sunk into some form of decaying waste. As he shuttered to imagine what kind of filth was underfoot, he began to hear meows and sensed a shifting movement in the room. Instinctively, he looked up to see what he guessed must be fifty to sixty cats. They were on the tables, on stacks of boxes, crawling on the cluttered couch, and among trash, food, and cans as far as the eye could see. They were in every unoccupied space. In other words, they were everywhere. Ironically, there were even cat litter boxes mixed in the heaps of garbage. As shocking as that should have been, the oddity could not outweigh the intensity of that smell! The strength of it suggested a combination of cat pee, feces, and cigarette smoke. The son had not exaggerated; this was bad. Matt silently questioned, *How could anyone live here?*

Matt shared a brief greeting with the son, but their eyes met without outward expression. After all, the mom was right there, and Matt did not want to be disrespectful. It was evident that the son felt the same need to be discrete, perhaps in an attempt to keep his mom from feeling embarrassed. *How could she not,* Matt wondered? He knew the answer, though. When he looked at her, he saw an overweight, unhealthy, older woman who was not living in the environment of a mentally stable person. Judging by the stacks of food and trash surrounding her, it looked as though she hadn't moved from her recliner for months. Still, Matt tried to maintain his composure, subdue the intense urge to vomit from the stench or to reveal, in any way, the level of his disgust.

But Matt had not forgotten how he'd gotten there and his feeling of excitement when he received the call. After months of continuous effort, his work started to pay off. Of course, he planned for this call to be the first of many. With that as his motivation, it wasn't difficult to push aside the distractions and began to focus on the task at hand. He needed to determine the cost of the repairs so he could make an offer on the offensive mess. If he priced it right, he would make money, and buying it would solve a massive problem for the son. It would be a big win for both of them. So, he went about his business, though every room he entered was more disgusting than the one before it. He pressed on undeterred until, at last, he finished the task.

There was no counter to the offer he made of $75,000. The son was just relieved that he could take only what his mom needed and walk away. Matt would clean up the rest, and the son could leave the mess behind forever.

Matt had to figure out how he would finance the deal. Given his current situation, he did not have the resources, but he would prove to be darned resourceful. First, he went to a hard money lender and secured a portion of the down payment. Then he talked to twenty or thirty people to see who was willing to invest their money for a return on that investment. After receiving several "no's," he persistently pushed on until he found a "yes" and someone willing to cover the down payment balance and the holding costs while he flipped the property. He was in business! Never once did he consider giving up until he received that yes.

Matt was ready to start clean-up and restoration. The cats were all relocated to either the SPCA or the humane society. However, the sad truth was that a few dead ones were underneath all of that trash. Several coats of paint were needed to get rid of the smell. It had leached into the walls so badly that some of the drywall needed to be ripped out.

After two months and $35,000 in restoration costs, Matt was finished. The fully-restored house sold for $225,000 after being on the market for only two weeks. In the end, after paying everyone off, Matt made more than $100,000, using none of his own money. (He teaches others his system in his 6 Figure Flipper course. See the details in the final score section of this chapter.)

Matt had never seen that kind of money before. He was energized! He knew that it was possible to find the next one and the one after that.

As of this writing, Matt has completed more than 200 flips through his investment company, called Vault Investment Properties. He has also invested in commercial properties, holds several single-family residences for rentals, and owns the Play Park Lodge in Lake Tahoe. He is thirty-three years old!

# CHOOSING THE RIGHT LIFE PARTNER

*"Who we marry is one of the most important decisions in life. One that will influence the level of happiness, growth, and success like no other choice."*

### ～ Nathan Workman

Matt met Marie through a mutual friend when he was twenty-three, and she was twenty-one. It was a brief introduction, but he was immediately captivated by her and wanted to ask her out. He emailed her a few days later, but she was skeptical of someone she didn't know asking her out by email, and said no. He tried a couple more times, and, after receiving positive reviews from a few friends who knew him, she finally decided to give him a chance.

Matt wanted to impress Marie and took her to a beautiful but pricy restaurant in downtown Sacramento called Ella's. His effort touched her heart, but he could have taken her to a less-costly place because it was Matt, not the restaurant, that she was impressed with. They both liked each other right away.

Both of them were facing challenges, and the timing wasn't the best for beginning a new relationship. Matt recalls, *"When Marie and I first started dating, I was just at the beginning of my journey as an entrepreneur. I was living at home, buried in debt, grinding eighty- and ninety-hour weeks, and was looking to find some stability in my career."*

Marie was working on her career as well and was studying to become a registered nurse. A nursing degree is challenging and requires a lot of committed study and concentration. Still, they made time for each other and were destined to fall in love.

Their wedding took place almost four years later, on October 8, 2016, on the water's edge at the Edgewood in Lake Tahoe. The location had a special meaning to them. Over the years, they had spent as much time as possible there and had fallen in love with the area. It was the perfect setting for their special day, and after the careful planning of every detail, the day had finally arrived.

Early afternoon at Lake Tahoe was approaching, and the sun's rays danced on the water behind the site of the ceremony. Positioned on the grassy area beyond a sandy beach stood a pretty, floral-adorned altar and neatly lined rows of guest chairs. Tall pine trees majestically surrounded the site, and the faded blue hills on the far side of the lake looked unreal and more like picturesque shadows in the distance. The peaceful Tahoe scene offered a beautiful and unique combination of a sunny beach setting with a touch of rustic coziness.

Matt, handsome in his blue tux, took his place by the altar, feeling like the luckiest guy in the world. He stood tall with his hands clasped in front of him, waiting in anticipation for his bride to join him.

Marie's fitted white dress was beautifully flattering. It hugged her to just above her knees, where it extended into a full skirt with a train of lace that gracefully swept the floor behind her. As she walked down the aisle towards her groom, a cool breeze lightly brushed her long dark hair. The length of it softly fell over her shoulders down to the middle of her back. She was stunning.

Matt took Marie's hand, and they greeted each other with a familiar and genuine love in their eyes. They continued to hold hands and faced each other while they said their heartfelt vows. The adoring crowd of family and friends erupted in cheers when they were pronounced husband and wife.

## LEADERSHIP – 6 FIGURE FLIPPER, MILLIONAIRE MINDCAST AND THE RICH LIFE ACADEMY

*"A Leader's job is not to do the work of others;*
*it's to help others figure out how to do it themselves,*
*to get things done, and to succeed beyond*
*what they thought possible."*

**~ Simon Sinek**

Just about everyone who knew Matt wanted to know how he was achieving such a level of success. The inquiries and requests for his time became overwhelming. Matt couldn't just teach one person at a time and still maintain a reasonable work schedule, but he wanted to help people. He needed to develop a way to do that and still be able to work. Matt decided to create an online course called the *6 Figure Flipper*. He could teach countless people at one time to learn how to flip houses.

At the same time, Matt started a podcast called *Millionaire Mindcast*. Its purpose was to help aspiring millionaires from all walks of life increase their income, impact, and influence. The focus would be on shifting people to an abundance mindset. He would interview and have conversations with people who were already in that mindset and had achieved an impressive level of success as a result. Matt's following was becoming huge. The plan was to reach that large audience so he could help them through his podcast.

As Matt began to acquire additional experience and connections, he developed a passion for helping people recognize the importance of living a full life. He understood that most people were so busy chasing money that they neglected other areas in their lives. He didn't have an issue with making a lot of money, but he knew that there was a lot more that contributed to living a RICH life—the letters of the acronym he developed. R.I.C.H. represents Relationships, Income, Contribution, and Health. Those are the pillars Matt feels that individuals need to concentrate on to live a full and balanced life. From there, he introduced the RICH Life Academy. It is a *"wealth building community of like-minded individuals looking to build their RICH LIFE through real estate."* (From the website)

*(You can find more on all of Matt's offerings in the "Final Score" section of this chapter.)*

## YOUR GAME PLAN:

Complete a review of your relationships. Are they creating obstacles that are keeping you from experiencing your desired success?

- Are you surrounding yourself with people who share your values and encourage you to reach your goals?

- How can you add more quality relationships to your life? Will you find a mentor or attend a conference? Maybe you will join a Mastermind?

- Tap into resources available to you to overcome the challenges in your relationships. See some suggestions in the "Winning Points" section below.

(Read the "Winning Points" below, then re-visit this exercise for any additions that the review of that section may prompt.)

## WINNING POINTS:

Matt is a young, recognized leader, and he is giving back in a big way! He is exceptionally charitable in his community and has students and followers from all over the globe. He has accomplished amazing success as a millennial entrepreneur and is more than willing to share his knowledge. Not only is Matt a multi-seven-figure real estate investor, but he teaches others through courses and podcasts as a business coach and speaker. He is the CEO of Vault Investment Properties, does a weekly podcast called the *Millionaire Mindcast*, and the founder of The Rich Life Academy, which is a personal development and accountability-based eLearning company that helps high achievers create more wealth, freedom, and fulfillment in their lives and businesses through real estate investing.

Full disclosure: I have personally taken Matt's *6 Figure Flipper* course. The tools and training are comprehensive and exceptional. Matt was also my coach when I did my first flip. I know that I would not have come close to the success I was able to achieve without his guidance every step of the way. It all goes back to his advice about finding a mentor. If your goal is to find success in an accelerated timeframe, do it! Find your Champion, no matter what industry you work in.

Matt's success is a real lesson in tenacity, growth, and giving back. He teaches that you don't always have to have the answers; you need to be diligent in finding them. *"Most people who don't think they have the answers right away walk away too soon,"* he says. Remember, Matt had no money when he got his first flip. But he relentlessly chased his goal and used all of his resources until he found success. He will tell you, *"Being resourceful is far more important than having resources."*

# MENTORS:

*"One relationship is literally all it takes to change your life. My very first mentor opened the door to another person who opened the door to another person. The sequence of events all started with one mentor."*

**~ Matt Aitchison**

A major takeaway from Matt's story is the importance of finding a mentor—and finding the right one. He says, *"Not only will the right mentor profoundly alter your mindset for the better, but they can shorten your learning curve, help you limit mistakes, and most importantly, push you to achieve success faster."* He also emphasizes that the experience he gained from working with them in the beginning gave him the confidence to pursue his first flip.

## MATTS FIVE STEPS TO FINDING THE RIGHT MENTOR

FROM HIS PODCAST, *MILLIONAIRE MINDCAST*:

1. **Get clarity** – Before you start to approach prospective mentors, be certain of your desired outcome. What specifically do you want them to help you with? What is this mentor going to bring into your life? Who has the results that you would like to replicate and model?

2. **Create your hit list of people who embody the qualities listed in step 1** – Who fits this profile?

3. **Value analysis** – How will you add value to your mentor? Yes, you read that correctly. Like all relationships, you cannot do all of the taking. You must be willing to give. Matt says, *"It's always important to make the deposit before you look for a withdraw."* The first mistake people make is to only think about what is in it for them. It is the quickest way to have that person close the door on you. For Matt, he offered to work for his first mentor for free while he learned because he had time that he knew his mentor didn't. So, he was adding value to the relationship. Ask your potential mentor how you can help them with something they are working on.

4. **How do you ask?** – Matt says this is the second mistake he sees people make. If the person you are looking at is highly successful, they likely have limited time. Separate yourself from others who wish to tap into their time. Ask them what it would take to earn five minutes of their time. It is not a yes or no question, and should be thought-provoking. Follow through with what they request. Matt says, *"You can provide and overdeliver if you have clarity on what would be worthwhile to them."*

5. **Building the relationship** – As with any relationship, it takes constant effort. Take action and show gratitude at every step. Matt adds, *"People who are highly successful want to help other people who want to be highly successful, but only if they are willing to take action."* Mentors love seeing results from their mentees. Matt says that it gets him fired up every time.

## CHOOSING THE RIGHT LIFE PARTNER:

Matt has a special relationship with his beautiful wife, Marie. When I asked him his thoughts on successful life partner relationships, he offered this advice.

*"When I get asked about my success formula, part of my equation is having a life partner who elevates your dreams and wants to help you build them instead of discouraging you from going after them. Having a partner that believes in you is a big success hack that many people overlook."*

- Choose a partner or spouse who aligns with the life and business you want to build.

- Don't be so focused on business or making money that you don't give your partner the attention they need and deserve. Matt says, *"Some people believe that they have to be focused solely on their businesses to become wealthy and to build their empires."*

- Understand the importance of choosing a supportive partner. Matt adds, "I understand from personal experience that having an extremely supportive partner can super fuel you. *Picking the right partner who is there for you emotionally, physically, and spiritually supercharges you* and *fills your emotional bank account. Your why becomes bigger."*

Matt emphasizes that you can share the highs and lows with the right partner and build that "Bigger Life" together.

## TOXIC RELATIONSHIPS:

*"Removing toxic people from your life will make room*
*for the right people to come into it.*
*You must be relentless in this to protect your environment.*
*It sounds ruthless, but toxic people have to go."*

**~ Matt Aitchison**

Much in the same way that Matt had to do a check on his high school and college relationships, everyone should review their peers and remove the toxic people from their lives. Matt also had a great family growing up. Unfortunately, that's not the case for everyone, and some of the poisonous people in their lives are their family members.

It doesn't matter where the problem relationships came from. To be successful and live our best lives, we need to follow Matt's advice and remove toxic people. If it is a family member, maybe the most that can be done is to put distance between the two of you. But the destructive influence of any problem individual must be removed.

We are adaptable to our surroundings, especially when it comes to the people we choose to spend our time with. Toxic people hold us back and keep us from reaching our full potential. Jim Rohn famously said, *"You are the average of the five people you spend the most time with."*

Matt says, *"If you are surrounded by nine millionaires, you will become the tenth."* For Matt, the millionaires he surrounded himself with were the GoBundance Mindcast members. His involvement with that group of mentors has been central to his growth. He adds, *"We grow into the conversations around us, so you have to be the gatekeeper of your relationships, conversations, and environments. Proximity is power and can work in your favor or can work against you."*

## THE MOST IMPORTANT RELATIONSHIP AND SELF FORGIVENESS:

*"The relationship you have with yourself has to be whole first before any of your other relationships can be whole.*
*You have to be the best, most aligned you.*
*Then, and only then, can your other relationships reach their maximum potential."*

**~ Matt Aitchison**

Being in jail and facing the possibility of returning there had been a hard lesson for Matt. He was committed to learning from the lessons; however, it was important not to allow the guilt to play any part in determining his future.

No one gets through life without facing some level of setback, hardship, or challenge. Maybe your past doesn't involve jail time. You have likely had to face other hard lessons yourself, though. The message is still the same. Your past doesn't equal your future! Use the lessons from your past to focus on building a better life. Surround yourself with quality people who you can learn from and will support you. Then forgive yourself and move on.

Matt was given a chance to plan a different future for himself after making his mistakes. He believes that he has an obligation to pay that gift forward. When you have the opportunity to hear him speak (put him on your calendar, because it is a gift), he almost always shares the story of his past in a way that benefits his listeners. He feels blessed to give back in a way that he would not have understood if it weren't for his experience and the challenges it brought into his life. Matt shares his story to give something back. He was inspired by being given a second chance—not once, but twice. He is tremendously grateful.

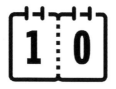

## FINAL SCORE:

Connecting with Matt is easy. He shares his success secrets and offers tools and training for those interested in leveling up in business and life.

Connect with Matt @ www.mattaitchison.com

- Learn more about Matt
- Find a link to the *Millionaire Mindcast* podcast

Join Matt each week for new insights as you march toward that million-dollar milestone and design your dream life.

- Book Matt for a speaking engagement

Check out the Rich Life Academy www.therichlifeacademy.com

*"The Next Generation of Real Estate Wealth Builders"*

- Become a member of the exclusive community
- Sign up for the *6 Figure Flipper* premium course
- Join an accountability group
- Sign up with Matt for one-on-one elite coaching

## FORWARD PASS:

*The next story about Mike Carney continues the discussion about the importance of solid relationships. His challenges are not as extreme as some others in the book. They more resemble those that are typically experienced every day by the average person. However, the lessons in his story are not any less important than the others. While we don't get to choose our parents, we certainly have the ability to choose how to be parents ourselves. We also have the choice to behave in a way that can positively influence the lives of others. Consideration, integrity, and character are all a part of Mike's life lessons.*

# MIKE CARNEY

---

# CHAPTER FOUR

# CHAMPION FATHERS, INFLUENCED LEADERS

*"Every father should remember that day his son will follow his example instead of his advice."*

**~ Charles F Kettering**

# MICHAEL CARNEY'S STORY
## VICE PRESIDENT, TEMPERATURE CONTROL DIVISION, STANDARD MOTOR PRODUCTS

Mike hurled the ball towards home plate, but the hitter didn't take the swing. He watched the ball sail past the batter and heard the stinging smack as it hit the catcher's mitt. The umpire shouted, "ball four!" It was the top of the last inning, and Mike's team was only ahead by one run. Crap! He'd just sent the tying run to first base.

The Little League coach, Mike's father, Art Carney, came out of the dugout to approach his son on the mound. *"You look tired,"* he said. *"You need to get the next hitter out or we need to make a change."* Mike could not think of anything worse than being yanked out of the game in the last inning. He wanted this win, or at least to be responsible for the outcome, one way or the other.

Focused and determined, Mike struck out the next two hitters. But the next batter made a play that no one expected when he hit a ground ball to the shortstop. It was an easy play that should have ended the game, except the shortstop bobbled the ball. There was just enough time for the guy who was on first to make it all of the way to third base, and, of course, the hitter was safe on first.

Mike stood alone on that mound in disbelief. The shortstop, who was usually surehanded, had made the error. But as promised, Art was already headed for the mound. Mike was beyond angry, knowing that he was about to be taken out for something that wasn't his fault. He didn't wait for the coach to reach him. He was so enraged that he threw the ball hard at his dad. Art caught the ball with a bare hand without even flinching. But there was no question by the stern look in his eyes that he found his son's act of defiance disrespectful and intolerable. *"Get off the field and go sit on the bench!"* he said firmly. It was at that very moment that the lesson began to unfold.

In Little League, everyone plays, but the weakest players usually end up on the bench by the end of the game. When Mike got tossed, Art had to send out one of the worst players on the team to take the open spot in the lineup. The replacement pitcher gave up a big hit on his very first pitch. Both of the runners Mike left on base scored, leaving his team behind by a run. Somehow, Mike's team got the last out and made it up to bat at the bottom of the final inning. The team loaded the bases, still trailing by one run, and as fate would have it, Mike's spot in the batting order was due at the plate. The chances were better than average that Mike would have brought at least one of those runners in with a hit. But his butt was on the bench, and the worst player on the team was up to bat in his place. Mike watched helplessly as the batter struck out on three pitches without ever once swinging the bat. Game over!

Mike hung his head in shame, knowing that he had disappointed his dad and let his team down. Even in his young eleven-year-old mind, he knew that his temper and the disrespect he'd displayed had cost the whole team. The second coach and several of his teammates also shared their frustration with Mike's behavior, but his father never uttered another word. He didn't need to. The look Art had given Mike on the field told him all he needed to know. He was destined to replay that moment in his head many times throughout the remainder of his life.

Art coached many of the Little League teams that his son played on when he was young. Mike began playing at the age of seven and continued to play competitively through the age of twenty-three. As a skilled pitcher, he threw hard and knew the game better than just about anyone.

Art was good at baseball himself but had been a huge local football star in high school. He could have had college opportunities, but he chose a different direction in his life when he married Mike's mom, Virginia (Jenny), his high school sweetheart. Mike felt that his dad would have liked him to work harder at football, as he played that sport too. But Mike didn't like that there was so much work to do for one game a week. He preferred baseball, and even though he suspected that it irritated his dad, he was fortunate that Art never pushed him in either direction. Instead, he allowed his son to make his own choices. Both Art and Jenny supported their son and his love for baseball.

Mike's dad was not the main disciplinarian in the family because he worked and was out of the house a lot. Though it was entirely possible to get stern discipline from either of his parents, Art was more of a life-lessons kind of dad, and he was a great teacher.

It was hard on Mike to know that he'd disappointed his dad. He would have much rather received any form of physical discipline than to know that he'd let him down. Art's life lessons made a huge impact on Mike's upbringing, however, and he certainly learned more than just baseball from them.

Art Carney worked his entire life in the automotive industry. He'd started as a teen working in a warehouse, pulling parts to fill orders. Over the years, he had grown through the ranks. At the age of thirty, he seized on an opportunity to become part-owner of an automotive distribution business located in southern Florida.

Mike started going to work with his dad at a young age. He thought it was cool to hang out with him and work among the other employees. Art simply wanted to teach Mike the value of hard work. Mike was ten years old and his dad kept him busy painting bathrooms and sweeping floors. It was three years before he was allowed to pick parts for orders or do anything that he considered to be one of the cool or fun jobs.

By the time Mike was old enough to drive, he had spent many weekends and summers working for his dad—when he wasn't playing baseball. In high school, he was recognized as one of the star players. He received publicity in local news articles and in other baseball leagues. But he was as smart as he was athletic, maintaining a 4.0 grade point average throughout school. Mike's work ethic was amazing even then. His dad certainly had a huge influence on that part of his character as well.

As he continued working for his dad, Mike was soon answering phones and working the counter, servicing customers. You could easily say he learned the business from the ground up, mostly because his dad created the educational atmosphere early in his life. The business had a distribution warehouse and nine stores. Mike wanted to work more independently and eventually got to work behind the counter and deliver parts at one of those stores. He continued working there until high school graduation. Then it was time to select a college.

As an athlete with a 4.0 grade point average, Mikes's athletic and academic achievements made him highly desirable. He was contacted by over a dozen colleges and junior colleges, including Duke and Cornell. The unexpected recognition was amazing, and Mike was shocked with every call or letter. But his excitement paled in comparison to how exceptionally proud Art and Jenny were of their son. The real surprise, however, came when the coach from the University of Florida called. Their baseball team was one of the best in the state, and it was an honor to get a call from a Division One college as a freshman. He ultimately decided to go there.

## COLLEGE AND THE FIRST JOB

*"It is in your moments of decision that your destiny is shaped."*

**~ Tony Robbins**

Mike started college at the University of Florida on a partial combined academic and baseball scholarship with the intention of majoring in engineering. But by the start of his fourth year, he discovered that juggling baseball and his studies was quite a challenge. Both required a lot of commitment, and he felt forced to choose between the two at times. One summer semester, he took a break from attending classes and instead decided to play baseball.

It was a decision that ended up leaving him short of the credits he needed to graduate on his original schedule. He never regretted the choice he'd made. It was a great summer, and he spent it playing in the sport he loved.

That summer also opened his eyes to the reality of athletics as a career. When he compared his own abilities to those of the players who succeeded at the highest levels, he knew he needed to be honest with himself about his future. It was time to concentrate on school and seek a realistic profession. He changed his major to business administration and graduated only three months later than he'd originally planned.

Mike graduated with a degree in business, but he also had completed several engineering courses before changing his major. The combination led to job interviews with several companies in a broad range of industries. Mike hadn't had any thought of returning to the family business or working in the automotive industry in any capacity for his first job. It wasn't until after receiving an official offer from Texas Instruments that his father asked him to consider one of the automotive industry's largest companies, Federal Mogul.

Mike went to Detroit and talked with several of the key executives at Federal Mogul. In that one visit, they convinced him that the company would be a great fit for him, and that he would have the opportunity to utilize the experience he'd already gained from working for his father. They offered him a job just outside Chicago, where he could earn his own "stripes." There, he would learn the manufacturing side of the industry, since his early experience had been geared more toward customer service and distribution.

It would be hard to move away from everything Mike had ever known in his life. But with the full support of his parents and the excitement of a new adventure, the final decision became an easy one.

Several years later, because his business partner became ill, Art decided he had to either assume sole ownership of the distribution business or sell it. But he did not want to take on the huge obligation without partnering in the business with either his son or daughter. Mike's sister had already made her career plans, and Mike discussed the possibility with his dad at length. But Mike didn't want to leave his new job, and in the end, they all agreed that selling the business was in everyone's best interest.

As heart-wrenching as it was to let go of the business, Art was most concerned about his forty-five employees. He never considered his own plans going forward until he found positions for everyone who wasn't retained by the new owners. He eventually completed the sale but stayed on until he was satisfied that all of his employees were secure in new jobs.

Art had always been known for putting others' needs ahead of his own, so it was no surprise when only a few years after the sale of the business, he and Jenny returned home to Georgia to help her aging parents. There, he took a general manager position with another automotive distributor just outside of Atlanta.

Meanwhile, Mike was thriving at Federal Mogul. He'd started out working in sales and was quickly recognized as a talented up-and-coming leader. The company had an aggressive manager training program for young recruits. After completing his assignment in Chicago, he was moved to Detroit to work in marketing. Soon after, he was transferred to product development and eventually landed with the acquisitions team. Federal Mogul only left their manager trainees in a specific position for a limited time before moving them because their goal was to teach them everything about the business as quickly as possible. Mike knew what he was signing up for and had to agree upfront to be moved around while he was in the development program. So, the next move was to Jacksonville, Alabama, as the materials and distribution manager.

All of this growth took place in a matter of a few short years. Mike proved himself to be an industry leader with an incredibly broad grasp and understanding of the industry. So much so that major players outside of Federal Mogul also noticed him. Many had been previous participants in the same aggressive development at Federal Mogul. One of the regional directors for Federal Mogul had moved on, but he hadn't forgotten Mike.

That regional director became the vice president for Hayden Incorporated, based in California, and he called to offer Mike a position on the West Coast in sales.

## FAMILY, GROWTH, AND CHANGE

*"Two things in life change you,*
*and you are never the same:*
*Love and Grief."*

### ~ Unknown

Mike was grateful to be surrounded by a very strong and supportive family when he was growing up. His parents were caring but firm, and his grandparents on both sides were also very involved in his life. He also had great support from a circle of cousins, aunts, and uncles. They were all important role models. The family environment created a strong foundation for him and helped promote his desire to be a parent and have a family of his own.

Mike experienced the joy of becoming a parent when his son, Matthew, was born while living in Detroit. Then he was blessed again when his beautiful daughter, Jenna, was born in Alabama. The two became the absolute loves of his life.

Constantly moving to learn and further his career had been necessary before he had children. His kids had changed everything, however, and moving around with a young family was becoming less and less desirable. He wanted to settle them into a more permanent setting while they were still small.

The new job offer had also come from California at a time when Federal Mogul was starting to encounter some growing pains. It was beginning to make more and more sense to make a change. After taking all things into consideration, Mike decided to accept the sales position and move his family to California. The vice president at Hayden Inc. was thrilled with his decision, and Mike started working for the company even before his move was complete.

Two divisions made up Hayden Inc.: automotive and industrial. These divisions served two distinctively separate markets. Mike's position, in keeping with his background, was with the automotive division. His sales territory was located throughout a large area of the West Coast, and he was taking it by storm. As in everything he'd done before, he was soon getting noticed for his extraordinary talent and work ethic. The parent company made some additional acquisitions and began moving around some of the corporate players. As a result, Mike was asked to fill a newly-created position as the Director of Marketing, and he could remain in California to take this promotion.

Working on the inside of the business, Mike's reputation as a leader continued to grow. For the next six years, he led his team to impressive levels of achievement. It was then that the parent company decided to sell the automotive division.

Four Seasons, a division of Standard Motor Products—a customer as well as a competitor—was the eventual buyer. They were located in Texas, but Hayden was so successful in California, they decided to leave the operation there under Mike's direction. The company, renamed Hayden Automotive, consolidated the manufacturing assets into their nearby distribution facility.

Two years later, Four Seasons was interested in snapping up another one of Hayden's competitors and bought a company called Eaglemotive. The new company was located in Texas, only a short distance from Four Seasons. It created an interesting dilemma. The question became whether Hayden would remain in California or if it was time to relocate them to Texas to operate in the same proximity.

Four Seasons asked the management teams of both Eaglemotive and Hayden to submit their best cases to keep the companies where they were already situated. They would leave one of the companies in place and relocate the other. Both teams were nervous, but it wasn't the first time the Hayden family had been tested. They worked hard on their presentation but knew the decision could easily go the other way. It was logical to move them to Texas. After all, Four Seasons was there, and the new acquisition was there too. But Mike and the management that he had assembled at Hayden had made an impressive name for themselves. In the end, Four Seasons decided to leave Hayden in place. It was unprecedented to keep Hayden as a stand-alone in California. But management didn't want to disrupt the company's extraordinary success or stall the growth plans that were already in the works.

While things were shifting in the business, Mike's personal life took an unexpected turn, and he became a single father of two. His children remained the light of his life. Nothing could ever change that fact.

Matt and Jenna were growing into normal healthy children. Matt was following in his father's footsteps with a love for baseball, and started playing T-ball when he was only five. Like his father, Mike coached the Little League teams that Matt would play on throughout his childhood years.

Jenna was all girl and had stolen her father's heart on the day she was born. She was always around Little League baseball by virtue of being dragged around with a baseball family. But aside from team events as a flag girl and in gymnastics, she tended to focus on typical girl interests and had a strong love for animals.

Mike was trying to manage a young and growing business when his life changed directions. But he was fortunate to have a strong circle of friends to support him and to work for a company that made the well-being of their employees a priority. The combination of the two helped him in both his professional and personal life.

Mike's friend, Debbie, was among the group of his long-term loyal friends. She and her daughter, Andrea, had also gone through some difficult changes, and she was sympathetic to Mike's challenges as a single parent. They had that in common. Having been friends for over a decade, they found it easy to confide in each other. Each of them trusted and appreciated the others' advice. Over time, their friendship grew into a close relationship. When it became evident that they should plan a future together, they became engaged.

Before their formal engagement, however, Mike experienced the toughest challenge he'd faced in his life. His father had been diagnosed with cancer, and despite an initial successful surgery, the cancer spread and eventually took his life at far too young an age. Mike not only lost his father, but he had also lost his mentor and friend.

Mike and Debbie planned their wedding on what would have been Art's sixty-fourth birthday. He wouldn't be there except in Mike's heart, but the date would forever mark the shared occasions.

 **FORWARD PASS:** *The following section of Mike's story is based more on a special memory than on a lesson on leadership and growth. The section was written for, and is dedicated to my beautiful friend Debbie Carney.*

## A NEW BEGINNING ~ A PERFECT DAY

*"Once in a while, in the middle of an ordinary life…*
*love gives us a fairytale."*

~ **Melissa Brown,** *Picturing Perfect*

It was late September, and summer had shifted into fall. In Southern California, the seasonal heat had given way to a more subtle warmth. It was a perfect day for a backyard wedding.

That wedding took place at the home of a couple who were very close friends of Mike and Debbie. The backyard was huge and felt like a tropical oasis, complete with tall banana and palm trees. The covered patio had enough room to place four large tables while leaving space for a dance area. Each table was draped to the floor with elegant white table cloths, and the centers were adorned with small silver vases filled with pink flowers.

At the patio's edge sat a circular bar covered by a thatched roof made from dried palm leaves. Directly in front of the bar was a separate table for the bride and groom flanked by two Ficus trees wrapped in brilliant white lights.

Floral pink candles floated in the clear glassy water of a small pool on the right side of the yard. Just beyond the pool's edge stood a lattice arch covered by gardenias and beautifully fragrant jasmine. It opened to a pathway leading to a raised wooden deck at the far corner of the property. In the center of the deck stood a gazebo that Mike had helped his friend build just a few days before. The gazebo columns and the deck's railing were adorned with white and pink flowers loosely wrapped in soft white tulle. That is where the ceremony would take place.

The officiant was an ordained minister and one of Mike's employees. It was typical for Mike to include someone he knew personally to make the occasion that much more meaningful. Raul was nervous about playing such a large role in Mike and Debbie's special day. *"After all,"* he said jokingly, *"how awful would it be to screw up my boss's wedding?"* Truthfully, he was extremely honored to be a part of the big day.

The sun dipped slightly to create a soft romantic sunlit setting. The guests gathered on the deck and below it in the surrounding grassy area. Anticipation, together with sincere happiness, filled the air. It was time.

Under the gazebo, Matt stood next to his dad along with Mike's best friend, Kevin. All of them looked handsome in their tuxedos. Debbie often chuckled that Mike was a bit of a fashionista, and the sharp white jacket paired with black slacks proved her point. Raul stood in position, looking to be in command and ready to do his part. Jenna and Debbie's best friend, Lyn, were pretty in pink as they walked down the pathway and gracefully took their places next to where the bride would soon be standing.

Debbie's daughter Andrea clutched her mom's hand as the two walked down the pathway together. Debbie was a lovely bride. Her blond hair brushed her shoulders, and the delicate skirt of her sleeveless white dress gracefully swept the floor with her every step. Mike didn't take his eyes off of his beautiful bride as she walked up the steps to join him. Andrea gave him Debbie's hand and stepped aside to watch with joy as her mom prepared to marry a man she admired and who would soon become her stepdad.

Surrounding the couple were forty of their closest friends and family, but once Mike took Debbie's hand, neither could see anything or anyone beyond the love they saw in each other's eyes. The sky was brilliantly lit with hues of yellow and orange as the sun began its descent. The setting was perfect.

Raul began to speak and then prompted the couple to affirm their love for each other with their vows. Then they exchanged their rings to signify an unbroken circle of love and commitment. They had traveled a long road full of unexpected twists and turns to arrive there. But God had a perfect plan. For the two of them, the world seemed to pause for a moment when Mike kissed his bride. It was as if to message God's approval as the two became one.

The music started, and the group of friends and family remained to joyfully celebrate with the newlyweds. The twilight was warm and wonderful, and the perfect day seamlessly drifted into a magical starlit night.

# LAST STOP TEXAS

*"Courage is the power to let go of the familiar."*

## ~ Raymond Lindquist

Hayden Automotive had survived two major changes due, in part, to Mike's superior leadership and the strength of his talented management team. Eight years after Four Seasons bought the company, however, the business atmosphere in California was showing signs of strain. The restrictions and regulations that had been taking place in the state over several years were making it increasingly difficult to rationalize maintaining the business in California. Also, there was the fact the parent company had operations in Texas and could effectively add Hayden to the existing infrastructure.

Worker's comp insurance, along with other costs of doing business as a manufacturer firm, was becoming excessive and untenable. Adding to the equation, Four Seasons in Texas moved a portion of its manufacturing activities to Mexico, creating a vacancy in a large section of the company-owned building. Finally, the lease on the building in California was coming up for renewal. With all of those factors, combined with an opportunity to improve efficiencies by combining the operations, the obvious decision was to merge the facilities.

Many of the Hayden employees had been with the company for over ten or even twenty years. That longevity said a lot about the admiration of Mike as a leader. Hayden simply did not experience the turnover that was normal for other companies. The Hayden group was a close-knit family, and they'd stuck together through many challenges over the years. Mike cared deeply for every one of them, and he knew that they would be heartbroken.

Years before, Mike witnessed his dad's commitment to the well-being of his employees when he was forced to sell his company. It is fitting to say that the apple didn't fall from the tree. Mike was determined in the same way to get the best deal he could for the Hayden employees. The company had been very successful and had a great reputation with the home office in New York.

The parent company had a reputation and long-standing track record for the generous treatment of employees affected by these types of difficult business decisions. The corporate and division leaders worked together with Mike to develop retention bonuses, offers for positions in Texas, and severance packages to benefit all of the 104 Hayden employees.

The night before the employee meeting was to take place, the vice president and human resource manager arrived in California for the meeting. Mike had dinner with them to discuss the meeting strategy. The VP offered to deliver the news to the employees, and Mike declined, telling him, *"No, the people need to hear this news from me."*

As the employees filed into the room, all eyes were on the front, where Mike stood with the visitors. Their curiosity piqued, knowing that the presence of the two Four Seasons executives likely meant that there was unusual importance to this meeting.

Mike scanned the room, looking into the eyes of many of the people he had known for years. The connection and commitment he felt were stronger than ever. He was a little anxious about delivering the message, but he was also confident that this was the right business decision. He hoped that they would not feel let down or in any way responsible for the decision to move the company.

But as he told them about the major change facing them, he did not see a lot of surprise on their faces. In truth, they had been surprised that the company was left in place for as long as it had been, and many commented later that it would have happened years earlier if it weren't for Mike and his management team. He had been their champion over the years, and they were still very much committed to him and the company. They would do their part.

The next several months were still difficult. The Hayden team was solemn at times and determined at others. They were as close as the family always had been. In the end, almost half of the employees relocated to Texas. Many of them maintained the exact positions they had held in California.

Putting his employees first, Mike's future with the company was still up in the air. He told the leaders that he wanted to remain with the company and assured them that he would do anything that they needed, including returning to a sales position. Shortly after the consolidation efforts had begun, Mike was offered a position as the general manager of the Temperature Control Division. Two years later, the vice president of the division was promoted, and Mike assumed that position. He became responsible for the operation as the Vice President of Temperature Control.

## A LEADER ADDRESSES CULTURE CHALLENGES

*"On a team, it's not the strength of the individual players, it's the strength of the unit and how they all function together."*

**~ Bill Belichick**

Long before he left California, Mike had an annual ritual of handwriting personalized Christmas cards to each company employee. Little did he know that the list would grow into hundreds after he arrived at Four Seasons. But he felt it was important to continue as it was his way of letting every individual know their efforts and contributions were noticed and appreciated. He wanted them to know that they were not just a number in a big corporation. The HR Department would run a list of Four Seasons Employees, including those in Mexico. If in the process, he ran across a name he didn't recognize, he made it a point to search out that person and learn something about them.

Four Seasons operations had two Texas Facilities: one in Grapevine and the other in Lewisville. Hayden had been a close-knit group, and Mike wanted that sense of cohesiveness to add value to the strong culture that already existed in the two locations. The fact that Standard Motor Products, the parent corporation, maintained a strong family-oriented approach to the business made the merger of Mike's California team, with its strengths, a perfect addition to the Texas operations.

In the beginning, Mike noticed that in the half-million square foot facility, the human resources department in Lewisville was located on the second floor in a remote corner. The majority of the employees in the facility worked in the warehouse, and the location didn't offer any privacy or convenience to them when they needed HR support. In addition, there was a security feature on the doors to the office area, which limited access without a manager scanning a card for entrance.

What was once a great idea for a safer environment had created an unintended roadblock for many of the company's employees. Mike first had the card swipe system deactivated during normal operating hours. Then later, during the reconstruction of the office facilities, he seized on an opportunity to relocate the HR Department to the first floor.

In addition to the structural improvements, Mike wanted to encourage a continued team, or family, atmosphere between the office and warehouse employees. Annual events such as celebration luncheons, awards presentations, and holiday parties had traditionally been held separately. The availability of an adequately-sized location as well as work schedule challenges had been obstacles to their success.

Mike thought that combining these events would allow the employees to get to know each other better in a relaxed setting, so he challenged the HR team to find adequate facilities so that all important company events could be enjoyed by all of the employees together. The effort was a big success.

But there had been other small hurdles.

In Mike's early days in Texas, one of his managers created an employee phone listing that had been given its own name and identity to distinguish one building from the other. In his mind, the manager felt it was a way to give his local employees a sense of identity. He felt the employees in the building across town didn't give his facility the attention it deserved. Over the next several weeks, the phone manual was redesigned to be more uniform with the sister facility.

Mike also started a trend of promoting or transferring people across both operations. The talent pool became well blended over the next few years. Eventually, the two facilities were fully integrated, and all of the employees resided under the same roof.

Mike observed, *"Cultural change and commitment can take a long time, but as it starts to develop, it typically gains speed and acceptance at an increasing pace."*

The improvements and cultural transition had begun several years before Mike and the Hayden team's arrival, but the addition of the new members and small, subtle changes kept the growth and development on track. The comradery continued to develop, and people were stopping and talking in the hallway.

Some leaders might think that time spent visiting is wasted time and maybe a little unproductive. Mike believed that as long as it didn't get out of hand, the hallway conversations created a healthy comradery and sense of inclusiveness. *"People that feel more involved and engaged are more likely to work together as a team. They take more pride in their work because they feel like their opinions matter,"* Mike said.

There are more than three hundred people working at Four Seasons as of this writing. Twenty-two of them celebrated twenty-five years of employment with the company in 2020. Mike sincerely values every one of them.

## YOUR GAME PLAN:

Are your leadership challenges keeping you from achieving your goals? Consider the following questions.

- Who are your influencers? Are you surrounding yourself with positive problem-solvers and mentors?

- Do you know how your employees feel about your leadership style? If not, you need to find out.

- What new skills do you need to learn to address your challenges? Where will you get that instruction? Books, mentors, podcasts, coaches, masterminds, classes? You guessed it, research these, and put together your game plan.

(Read the "Winning Points" below, then re-visit this exercise for any additions that may be prompted by the review of that section.)

## WINNING POINTS:

*"I try as hard as possible to be kind and positive
towards everyone. However, I also make sure that the people
I choose to associate with and spend my time with
are people of character. I try to tolerate everyone
but surround myself with positive influence whenever possible."*

### ~ Michael Carney

Mike's story certainly demonstrates how you are influenced by every relationship in your life. Being choosey about the people you surround yourself with is critical to your success. It is a familiar theme that I have found consistent with every successful individual whose story I have had the honor to write. But Mike's story is also a story about character, integrity, and that old-fashioned Golden Rule. We all learned as children how to treat people. How you do this is a reflection of your values and speaks volumes about you. I believe Mike has the concept engraved in his very being.

Finally, Mike's story is about possessing and maintaining a great work ethic. He was lucky to have a dad to show him some of the ways. But he picked up a lot on his own too.

*"Being involved in sports my whole life set the competitive and team-oriented aspects of my personality. That is why I could never support participation-only types of awards."*

**~ Michael Carney**

Working hard to get out from under his dad's reputation to make a name for himself taught him that hard work could take him anywhere he wanted to go. Mike certainly worked hard and had a strong drive.

When I asked Mike about his drive, and what his big "why" was, this was his answer:

*"I don't know why I am driven, other than it makes no sense to me to exert effort towards anything if you aren't going to give it your best and try to win. I just don't think that being average is okay. I read somewhere once that, "you really never get a chance to do anything on earth a second time." It took me a long time to understand that because you really can do most things again, but it's a fact that you will never get another first time. Doing anything half-ass or partially just seems like a waste of what God gave us, what our parents and teachers tried to teach us, and what people who depend on us deserve."*

Finally, as a matter of full disclosure, I met Mike almost thirty years ago when he hired me to work in his marketing department at Hayden Inc. He was my boss for about six years. I was one of those employees who made the move across town when Four Seasons bought the company. I know firsthand what it is like to work under his leadership. I believe it is a leadership style that should be practiced by anyone responsible for managing people at any level.

*"Most managers make rules
and expect their employees to adapt to their management style. I
am a firm believer that great leaders
adapt their style to their people.
People are different, and not all are motivated
by the same things. At the end of the day,
it's about giving a damn about people."*

~ **Michael Carney**

## MANAGEMENT AND LEADERSHIP

After his years of experience Mike doesn't use the title of "manager" much anymore. He talks about what he feels the differences are between a manager and a leader.

He said, *"It is amazing how many good managers there actually are. What I am talking about are actual managers who are not necessarily leaders. Managing can be applicable to a project, one's time, a schedule, or even people who are spectacular parliamentarians. Yet, no matter how good an individual is at managing activities or events, it doesn't seem to always equate to them having the skills of a good leader. I try to focus on helping people home in on their leadership skills or make sure good managers get put in positions where their managerial talents can be utilized. But those managers may not be the ones I want to see lead others."*

**To illustrate the difference between a manager and a leader, Mike shared one of his favorite quotes:**

*"You cannot manage men into battle.
You manage things; you lead people."*

~ **Grace Hopper (retired Admiral, U.S. Navy)**

## MIKE OFFERS SOME LEADERSHIP ADVICE

- **Treat people like adults and trust in them until they prove you wrong.** Don't micromanage them. Ownership and achievement are huge motivators.

- **Don't dwell on failures.** Recognize the lesson, but do not hold onto the failure long term. Mike said, *"Our failures and shortcomings always seem to stick in our minds forever, but somehow the greatest times are harder to lock into our memory banks. It just makes sense to let go of negative thoughts so that they don't block out the good."* Make this a practice for yourself and allow your people to learn their lessons and move on as well.

- **Be an optimistic leader.** Mike shared his thoughts on this. *"I believe people are good and want to succeed, so I approach everything from a glass half-full perspective. Many enter into relationships more skeptical than I do. For me, it works best to be upbeat, positive, and to anticipate success."*

Years ago, Mike was attending an All-Star Manager preparation meeting for Little League. The instructor asked the room two questions. The first was, *"How many of you have lost a game you should have won?"* Everyone in the room raised their hands. He then asked, *"How many of you have won a game you should have lost?"* Everyone in the room raised their hand—except Mike. The instructor looked quizzically at him and might have even been a bit miffed. He asked, *"You have never won a game where you were the underdog and should have lost?"* Mike stood up and answered. *"No, sir, because I have never entered any game or competition with the thought or attitude that I couldn't win. Nor will I teach kids they are so overmatched that they have no chance."* Hence one of many reasons that Mike always tries to be upbeat and positive.

- **Don't lie to your employees.** There are going to be things that you can't tell them. It's perfectly okay to tell them you can't answer them. But don't lie to them. And never lie *for* them.

- **Don't ask people to do things that you aren't willing to do.** As a leader, the example you display by your actions is far more impactful than your verbal direction could ever be.

- **Maintain your integrity.** When you lose your integrity, there is nothing left of the respect your employees may have had for you.

Mike's dad once told him that he never once looked in the mirror and didn't like the guy looking back. Yes, it is somewhat of a cliché by today's standards. But to Mike growing up, it was another one of those valuable lessons on integrity that he never forgot. *"If you don't like yourself, you cannot successfully lead people,"* Mike said.

- **People most often do what they are rewarded for doing.** Many times, you don't even realize you built a reward structure. Mike emphasized that you need to be careful of the reward structure that you implement, or you may see the behavior opposite of what you desire.

**Mike shared a funny story to illustrate his personal experience.**

Some time ago, the company was experiencing an unusually large demand for their products, and Mike had to request a seven-day workweek for a short time. Understandably, some of the employees wanted to go to church on Sunday. He made a deal with them to come in at 6 a.m. and leave at 10 a.m. so that they could still make it to church. "I just want all of the hours I can get, so I will compromise," he told them. *"I think I converted half of my employees to Christianity,"* he said, laughing. *"All of a sudden, everyone wanted those hours so that they could go to church."* He could have easily asked them to temporarily choose an evening time to attend church. He also could have asked them to go to church and then come back in the afternoon to finish their shift. Very few of them would have chosen that option.

Mike became aware of the reward concept after reading the following book that he highly recommended as one of his favorites:

*The Greatest Management Principle in the World*, by Michael LeBoeuf, Ph.D.

The principle is that people will always do what you reward them for. In chapter two of his book, the author gives several common examples.

- ○ The company wants loyalty but pays the highest salaries to the newly hired or the employees who threaten to leave.

- ○ The company wants to promote cost savings but gives the larger budget increases to those who exhaust their resources.

- ○ The company wants quality work but sets unreasonable deadlines.

By now, you get the idea. The bullet points above only represent a few of the examples the author highlights in his book. It is worth your time to buy the book and read it in its entirety. Over the years, Mike has given copies of the book to many of his employees in management or leadership roles.

- **Seek out mentors, but choose them carefully.** Mike reiterated the message Matt gave us in the previous chapter on mentors. There are just as many poor choices as there are good. Be certain that anyone you shadow or take advice from is in sync with your values.

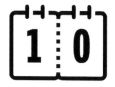

## FINAL SCORE:

Because of the huge demand for Mike's time, he is private about his contact information. However, if you have a question for him or would like to invite him to speak to your group, please email me at karen@karenhunsanger.com, and I will get your message to him.

## FORWARD PASS:

*The two stories included in the Halftime Report will take us on a short break from the more personal life event stories. (Don't worry, we will return to some great ones in the Third Quarter.)*

*In this section, I wanted to focus on using teams as a champion resource in overcoming obstacles and in problem-solving at work. Challenges at work can often be more easily tackled by utilizing the diverse set of ideas and talents offered by a team. Let's take a look.*

# HALFTIME REPORT

## CHAMPION TEAMS

*"It doesn't make sense to hire smart people
and then tell them what to do; we hire smart people
so they can tell us what to do."*

**~ Steve Jobs**

## HALFTIME CHAMPION QUALITIES:

* Empowerment      * Giving Back      * Achievement

* Appreciation      * Quality      * Productivity

* Happiness      * Investing in others growth and success

# TED AND KAREN
# HUNSANGER

## HALFTIME REPORT

---

# CHAMPION TEAMS

*"Great things in business are never done by one person. They're done by a team of people."*

**~ Steve Jobs**

# TED HUNSANGER
## THE YEAR 1995 –
## PRODUCTION MANAGER, HAYDEN INC.
*(Some names have been changed)*

Though it would have been commonplace in Southern California, the unsettled feeling in the building wasn't because of an earthquake. Carol, the manufacturing manager, was walking around the plant, and the air felt undeniably shaky. Every employee within Carol's proximity shuddered in her presence. Not an eye wandered from the task in front of them for fear of drawing her unwanted attention.

Carol had a short, stocky build and carried herself with an outward toughness that often made people feel like she could take them down with a single punch. Of course, she never hit anyone, but her look was fierce, and the way she managed her employees was old school and reliant on sheer intimidation. She offered no apologies for her tough management style. It was how things were done when she was coming up through the ranks.

Ted was one of the three shop foremen who reported directly to her, and he had felt her wrath on more than one occasion. One time, she received word that he'd complained about her to someone. He soon found himself working on the floor for a week at a menial and physically demanding task. He didn't make that mistake again.

Ted had worked with Carol for about ten years and became one of a few to witness her in a different light. She had a compassionate side that was rarely seen—and certainly never before a person earned her trust. Carol *did* trust Ted. Despite never having kids or ever being married, she loved Ted like the son she never had. But it was a conditional love.

Carol walked through the plant en route to her office for the weekly meeting with her management team. They were already in the room when she entered. As usual, there were donuts available for all in attendance, and one of the newer staffers nervously rushed to set Carol's favorite on the table next to her. Carol never even acknowledged her, and Ted smirked at the spectacle from where he was seated across the table.

Sitting three or four seats down on Carol's right was another foreman named Dave. He was known for his smart-ass comments and the quivering of his bottom lip whenever Carol called him out. Still, he seemed to get a great deal of satisfaction from her disparaging replies.

Carol had barely begun speaking when Dave interrupted with one of his sarcastic comments. Almost everyone in the room started to chuckle, but some sat quietly, smiling, knowing that there would surely be a swift response. They were right. Without ever looking up from the paperwork on the table, Carol grabbed her donut and hurled it sideways with precision in Dave's direction, catching him square in the side of his face. As if in slow motion, it exploded on impact, and pieces of it hung from his glasses before finally falling onto the table and floor. Dave didn't flinch and instead simply grinned as if pleased with himself. When his bottom lip began to quiver, the room erupted in howls and laughter.

The vice president of operations was not as amused when he heard the story. The truth is that he and Carol had gone toe-to-toe many times over the years regarding her unorthodox management style. He was becoming tired of the constant fight.

Some months later, the company's distribution center was separated from manufacturing and relocated to a different facility across town. The building was no longer big enough to house the combined operations. Carol, who had run both, was moved to manage the new warehouse. Ted then assumed a production manager position, reporting directly to Don, the vice president of operations.

Don had been concerned about the training and influence that Ted received from Carol over the years. During Ted's tenure, she had been his only mentor. Don was also worried about Ted's future. He was a young manager and deserved some solid training. He knew that it would not benefit Ted or the company if Carol's tyrannical management style remained after her departure. Don had done some research and was intrigued by a management program he came across that stressed team development. He was anxious to give the employees a positive, new environment. So he sent Ted to that supervisory team-building training.

On his way to the week-long training, Ted felt eager to learn something new. But he was also skeptical. He'd been to many seminars over the years that pumped people up while they were there, only for that enthusiasm to be left behind when they left. In previous workshops, he'd witnessed the lessons being forgotten once back at the office, making the training a waste of time. He wasn't convinced that this would be any different.

Ted was pleasantly surprised when these team-building classes began, however. This training was different from any he'd attended before. It was comprehensive and engaging. The week went by fast, and he felt like he had taken away quite a lot of value.

Don was determined to create a team culture within the company. He wanted the employees to begin feeling appreciated. When Ted returned, he asked him to write a report on what he'd experienced and to detail the lessons he'd learned while they were still fresh. Once Ted started to put pen to paper, he realized just how much he had taken away from the training. He was more eager than ever to begin putting that training to work.

Don was so impressed with what he'd read that he told Ted it was time to implement the team concept. Once word got out, the naysayers also came out. Don and Ted were not deterred.

# THE TEAMS PROJECT

*"When the team is directly involved
in their own process improvement, it improves skill,
quality, morale, and increases productivity.
They are the experts and understand
better than anyone where the hiccups are."*

## ~ Ted Hunsanger

Ted began to selectively build his team. He was careful to choose a group that he felt would participate and work together with respect for each other's ideas while remaining open to change.

Every individual had only been trained to perform at one job with no knowledge or understanding of the processes that either proceeded or followed their own. They never strayed from their assigned posts on the manufacturing assembly line, creating a bottleneck when one function was operating out of sync with another. At times, some stations were frantically working while others were unproductively waiting for them to catch up.

The first thing Ted did was to cross-train the employees so they could move to the different stations to help each other out. No one would be standing around, and if a problem occurred with one process, there was additional labor working to solve it quickly.

Next, he addressed the productivity of those individual stations to perfect the timing and eliminate the bottlenecks so that there was a constant flow from start to finish. That is where the team concept would become magic.

In the past, any changes to productivity and process had always been dictated by management. Ted called the team together and challenged them to review their processes and make suggestions for improvements. Each task would affect the next in line, so they would need to work together to keep from inadvertently creating problems for each other. They were extremely excited and enthusiastic. They were being acknowledged for their expertise, and for the first time, they felt valued.

The first thing they tackled was the layout of the operation and created a workflow that made more sense. Next, the team dissected each process and came up with ways to cut out wasted time. The only time they involved maintenance or engineering was when they needed expertise in those areas. Once those departments were engaged, however, they instinctively wanted to take over the project. But Ted put his foot down on behalf of his team, and Don backed him up. The departments from the outside were utilized for their part and then politely asked to leave.

Throughout the process, there was much skepticism. In fact, it was not always smooth sailing within the team itself. There were times when the difficulties were overwhelming, and even Ted questioned the worthiness of the project. But Don could see the progress they were making and encouraged Ted to continue.

The team had been given a ninety-day window to complete the entire project. They were to increase productivity by twenty-five percent and realize a $750,000 savings for the company. When they were finished, they had a thirty percent improvement with $1.2 million savings for the company. The project was a huge success. It was so successful that Ted received an award in recognition of his accomplishment. Don instructed the remaining manufacturing operations to work with Ted and his team to make their improvements.

As of this writing, that project was completed twenty-six years ago. Ted has successfully used his training and expertise with dozens of teams since then. He has never forgotten the value of recognizing and involving individuals and how an efficient team can contribute to the overall success of a company.

HALFTIME REPORT CONTINUED

# A TEAMS VOICE

*"If you lead a team, start asking questions and really listening.
Start valuing the contribution
of your teammates ahead of your own,
and remember that when the best idea wins,
so does the team."*

**~ John C. Maxwell**

# KAREN HUNSANGER

## THE YEAR 1996 –
## DISTRIBUTION MANAGER, HAYDEN AUTOMOTIVE

*(Some names have been changed)*

I looked up from my desk to see a group of about ten distribution employees marching into my office. They filed in one by one, each looking as determined and defiant as the next. It was apparent that they had some sort of grievance.

I had just accepted the position of distribution manager a few weeks earlier. The company was sold and had split its industrial and automotive divisions. I moved along, with the automotive group, across town into the company's existing distribution center. My manager (Mike Carney, chapter 4) asked me to take the position because he felt I had the skill to implement the changes we would need to make in the transition.

The team members in my office were not new to their positions. Most had worked in the distribution center for years. But I was new to them, and they were not immediately sold on me as their new leader. They found many interesting ways to test my skill in those first few weeks.

The ringleader of the group in my office was the shipping clerk, Ronny. I soon learned that he was known to insert himself into any situation that would cause a commotion or simply award him the center stage. It turns out that this particular protest was about a decision affecting the packaging department. It wasn't even within a hundred feet of Ronny's area in the building. He'd gone so far as to organize a crowd of workers that included people from receiving and a handful of material handlers. None of them had anything to do with packaging. But they were either being protective of one of their own or wanted to be in on the dissent.

Standing meekly in the very back of the room was Verna. She was quiet and sweet and the fastest fan clutch packager in the department. She wasn't one to complain, so I was certain that she had not instigated the protest. It was more likely that she'd voiced her displeasure with a new packaging procedure, and Ronny took the ball and ran with it. If anyone in the group were to have a genuine concern on a packaging issue, it would be Verna. Her presence with this raucous group was out of the ordinary, and it grabbed my full attention.

A week earlier, a packaging expert had come from the main office in Texas to review our fan clutch packaging process. He quickly observed that our work tables were not as efficient as they needed to be. At approximately ten feet in length, he said they were too long. Verna would completely line the top of the table with rows of boxes, travel the distance dropping in the product, and then make another run to drop in a packet of instructions. Finally, she would go the distance again to label, close the boxes, and load them into shipping containers. The expert said that traveling the ten-foot span that many times was costing valuable time. He developed new five-foot tables with bins on an upper shelf that held all of the components required to go in or on the boxes with the product. The concept was to eliminate the ten-foot runway and instead have everything within arm's reach. Saving the steps would, in turn, save time.

Verna had been working with the old process for years, she was comfortable with it, and she was lightning fast. Nobody had asked for her input or opinion, and she wasn't happy about the change at all. Verna sincerely believed that she was packing more products the old way. Her speed had earned her a reputation as the best, and she was willing to fight to protect it.

So, here before me stood Ronny and his posse, voicing their disapproval of the new process. Even Verna was standing a little taller than I had ever noticed before. After all, who did that so-called packaging professional think he was? Our packers were the real experts. They had been doing the job for years.

Without getting out of my chair, I leaned back and looked sympathetically at the stern faces in front of me. All at once, I understood the fact that no one had included them or asked for their expertise. They were right to feel slighted. At the same time, I smiled, knowing that the expert was right, and I knew that I would have to convince this group that he was right too.

*"Let me get this straight,"* I started. *"You guys feel confident that the old way of packaging is faster, and you don't approve of the change."* Almost in unison, the group gave me an emphatic *"Yes!"* So, after a moment of thought, I reached into my desk drawer and grabbed a stopwatch. *"Okay,"* I said. *"This is what I think we should do."*

Every eye was on me, and I could see the intrigue on their faces as I continued. *"I think you should conduct your own experiment. Verna, you go and pack at each of the stations, first one and then the other. Be sure you are at your top speed at both. Ronny, you time her and count how many fan clutches are packed during the same amount of time at each station. I'll tell you what. If, in the end, you determine that the old method is faster, we will continue using it. The decision is completely up to you."* I knew I was taking a risk. But I was also confident in what they were about to discover. The big difference was that now that they were included in the decision, they would own the new packaging method.

I watched as the mood in the room completely shifted. There was excitement at the challenge and an actual spring in Ronny's step as he exited. They'd won and were going to prove their point.

It was about an hour later when the group returned to my office. This time they filed in a little more slowly, and they were smiling almost reservedly. Ronny was at the helm again as he spoke for the group. *"The expert was right; the new procedure is faster,"* he admitted. I turned to Verna and asked her, *"So do you want to use the new workstations?"* She nodded enthusiastically. Ronny continued with the group's recommendation that all of the old tables should be replaced by the new ones as soon as possible.

I got up from my chair to address them. I congratulated the team and told them that I was proud of their accomplishment. But the truth is that I learned more from them that day than they learned from me. Undoubtedly, the exercise boosted my credibility with them a bit. But more importantly, my focus shifted squarely to their welfare. From that moment on, they had input on any decisions within their work areas. I also encouraged them to cross-train in other jobs they were interested in to create a happier and more engaged team and develop better coverage and expertise in all areas within the distribution center.

The team's comradery was strong before I arrived there, and I did my best to make sure it continued during my tenure. But it was witnessing their growth and commitment that made my efforts so rewarding.

## YOUR GAME PLAN:

(A **TEAM** is a joining of forces to achieve a common goal.)

Could a team of specialists collectively help solve the issues keeping you from reaching your corporate or entrepreneurial goals?

- Define your goal or problem. Then make a list of people who could join forces and have the combined skills to reach a desired solution or outcome.

- Read about working with teams in author Matthew Overlund's book, *Stop Pulling the Ship*. (See Matt's story in Chapter 7.)

There are six areas Matt explores in his book in the section entitled Transforming Your Team.

- Read *From Supervisor to Super Leader,* by author Shanda Miller. It is an invaluable tool that answers many questions on the topic of teams. (See more on this author, her website, and her leadership courses in "Winning Points," below.)

- What new skills do you need to learn to develop an effective team? Where will you get that instruction? Books, mentors, podcasts, coaches, masterminds, classes? Do your research and put together your game plan.

(Read the "Winning Points" section below, then re-visit this exercise for any additions that the review of that section may prompt.)

## WINNING POINTS:

You may have noted the shared last name of the individuals in those two stories. Ted and I are happily married, and as of this writing, it has been a joyful (mostly) twenty-seven years. We have learned many valuable lessons from each other on this topic and have engaged in numerous lively discussions. It has been an amazing journey.

Both of us agree that a team's success is built on a foundation of solid relationships and effective communication. There has to be a level of trust and comradery among the leaders and individual members. Strong team leadership must also communicate goals and objectives, and all team members are encouraged to express ideas and concerns freely. Above all, everyone on a team must feel valued and at the same time appreciate and remain open to the ideas and opinions of the other members.

In her book, From Supervisor to Super Leader, Shanda Miller says, "Building a relationship and trust with each team member does not happen overnight. Think of each relationship as a long-term investment that begins with building the relationship and continues with ongoing nurturing." She says that the best way to get to know someone is to ask them to share their life story—and share yours in return. But Shanda cautions, "While your team member is sharing, it is important that you suspend judgment, show empathy, and focus on listening."

## EXTRA POINT:

Connect with author **Shanda Miller:**

- Become a Super Leader: www.becomeasuperleader.com

*"Intentional Leadership for Building High-Performance Teams."* (Taken from the website)

From the menu you can find a copy of her book and learn about her courses:

○ Team Builder Course

○ Purpose-Driven Productivity Course

○ Project Management for Supervisors

# ENTREPRENEURIAL TEAMS

The main difference between building a corporate team versus one for an entrepreneur is in the leadership itself. A corporate leader has the safety net of an establishment behind them, whereas an entrepreneur is on their own. Being the sole risk-taker means that an entrepreneur's team-building skill is vital to their long-term success.

Outside of leadership, the concept for building teams remains the same for both. They are both dealing with people, and along with that comes the need to build solid relationships and communicate with proficiency.

The other main difference may only be in the number of people on the team and their specialties. Some entrepreneurs only have outside team members (including start-ups) that consist of professionals like CPAs and attorneys. Unlike traditional teams, they may only meet when there is a joint problem, such as a tax issue that is also a legal matter.

Some entrepreneurs have an outside team known as an advisory board. These are not to be confused with the board of directors, a formal group that the shareholders elect. An advisory board is an informal group that is appointed by the CEO to council the business leaders. They tend to be more budget-friendly and consist of a trusted group of people with various specialties and viewpoints. Some may be industry insiders or even mentors that can fill in the gaps between the leaders' strengths and weaknesses.

Entrepreneurs who have an inside team may employ people with specialties such as marketing, sales, or bookkeeping. There are often team members that wear multiple hats. Ensuring that everyone on the team is focused on the same goals is still as critical as in any other business.

When looking at the various types of teams, building strong relationships, offering support, and communicating the company objectives and goals matter whether you are an entrepreneur or a corporate leader.

## SELF-DIRECTED WORK TEAMS –
## SEMI-AUTONOMOUS TEAMS

The "self-directed work team" has become an increasingly popular concept in various businesses over the past several years. In reality, the name is a little misleading. In his book, *Leading Self-Directed Work Teams*, Kimball Fisher states that a more fitting title might be "High-Performance Teams." Teams still need infrastructure and coaching, so a level of supervision and management is still necessary. The author explains that the concept of self-directed teams does not eliminate management; it merely changes its role.

In this model, management shifts from being the driver of productivity to a role of supporting it. In turn, the function of the team becomes more influenced by the customer and less by management. Just how difficult is it for management to relinquish some of its power? I see some potential difficulties with such a drastic mindset shift on behalf of a headstrong management structure. Also, it seems that each individual's communication skills and strengths would need to be exceptional. Success then depends on effective training at all levels to become a priority. Kimball Fisher tackles these questions and a variety of others. His book is an exceptional resource if you are considering the development of a new team structure.

Ted's team was a semi-autonomous group of high performers. He handpicked each of them with a specific strength in mind. Also, as the production manager, he still managed the hiring, firing, and scheduling of the team. But the company leaders above him still had limited input, concentrating primarily on providing financial goals and performance expectations, and Ted struggled with upper management wanting to take over the process. But once he succeeded at keeping them at arm's length, the team's success was extraordinary. They performed well beyond the expectations of management.

Given the right balance of empowerment and structure, a team is an invaluable asset.

## IN THE END ZONE:

Ted and I firmly believe that including teams in decision-making and process improvements is unbelievably advantageous and can touch everyone in an organization. First of all, empowering people, teaching them new skills, and giving them the ability to achieve more success has no greater value or reward. People who are engaged feel more appreciated, happy, and are more productive. That equates to more freedom for managers who are not dealing with minor issues daily. Finally, when the team is laser-focused on productivity and quality, management is happy with the resulting cost savings and improved customer satisfaction. It is a win-win!

*"The courage of leadership is giving others the chance to succeed even though you bear the responsibility of getting things done."*

**~ Simon Sinek**

## FINAL SCORE:

To contact either of the Hunsangers you can email us at karen@karenhunsanger.com

## FORWARD PASS:

*Get ready for an emotional experience! The powerful stories coming up in the Third Quarter tell how two ordinary people faced extremely challenging life circumstances. Jennifer Fike and Jason Koger were confronted with incredible difficulty in their lives and overcame with the courage and faith of the Champions that they are.*

---

# THIRD QUARTER

## FAITH AND PERSEVERANCE

*"Faith and perseverance are the key to overcoming obstacles."*

**~ Lorna Jackie Wilson**

THIRD QUARTER CHAMPION QUALITIES:

* Perseverance          * Commitment          * Triumph

* Faith          * Grit: (courage, resolve, strength of character)

# JENNIFER FIKE

# CHAPTER FIVE

---

# GRIT

## (COURAGE, RESOLVE, STRENGTH OF CHARACTER)

*"I survived because the fire inside me
burned brighter than the fire around me."*

**~ Joshua Graham**

# JENNIFER FIKE BSN, RN, SCRN

## RN, SAN ANTONIO REGIONAL HOSPITAL; CLINICAL INSTRUCTOR, LOMA LINDA UNIVERSITY SCHOOL OF NURSING

*"Jenn, the baby is having a seizure!"* Jennifer sat down hard on the concrete step beneath her. Her heart sank as she grappled with the words she heard over the phone from her mother-in-law, Cindie. Jennifer was in Texas, miles away from her two-year-old son, Ethan, who was being cared for by his grandparents in Southern California. She knew Cindie was calling her from a hospital because she could hear the beeping sound of a monitor intermingled with the frantic movement of the medical staff in the background. She sat helplessly listening to her small son seizing and gasping for every breath as his tiny diaphragm struggled against the convulsing assault.

Jennifer was in shock. How could this be happening? Her mind was consumed with the horrific thought that she might hear her baby die over the phone. The combined guilt and grief were overwhelming. She was heartbroken that she wasn't there to comfort and fight with him, and she prayed that he would not give up as she listened. *"C'mon, Baby,"* she coaxed under her breath with words he could not hear. She felt powerless and wanted more than anything to touch him from a distance and send him the strength to pull through.

Cindie was shifting between reporting to her on the phone and speaking to some of the muffled voices in the background. Jennifer didn't know if Cindie was even aware that she had spoken out loud. But Cindie's voice sounded defeated as she whispered under her breath, *"I don't think he is going to make it this time!"*

Jennifer gasped. Cindie was there and could see what Jennifer could not. The thought that she might believe that things were going to end badly was terrifying.

It was not Ethan's first seizure. He had a frightening history, having his first when he was only four months old. In the first year after his birth, Jennifer and her husband, Anthony, had called 911 thirteen times in fear for his little life. By the time Ethan was two years old, he had suffered hundreds of seizures, and his parents struggled to find medical professionals who knew how to control them. During that second year, there were not as many hospital visits but only because they were learning to manage the seizures better at home. They began to realize that the doctors weren't doing anything different at the hospital than they could do themselves. But the episodes were still frequent and came on with little warning.

Jennifer and Anthony were in Texas for the wedding of Anthony's high school best friend, Jon. They had not left home for any length of time and certainly not gone any distance in two years. There were not many people the baby could be left with. But Cindie was the director of an emergency room and critical care unit in a San Bernardino hospital. She was better equipped than most to handle a medical situation.

Both Anthony and Jennifer were in the wedding, so they flew out a couple of days early. Anthony's parents, Pat and Cindie, rented an RV to drive to Texas from Southern California for the wedding. They were going to take their time with Eden, Jennifer's four-year-old daughter, and two-year-old Ethan. In route, Pat and Cindie had stopped to spend the night at their vacation house in Arizona. Just as they were about to set out again, Ethan began to seize.

Jennifer and Anthony were in an auditorium the day before the wedding at an event for the bride-to-be when Jennifer's cell phone rang. She looked at her phone and realized the call was coming from her mother-in-law, Cindie, so she hurriedly left her seat and rushed outside to answer it away from the noise.

Jennifer was stunned by Cindie's account. She was almost numb, *"Dear God, how is this happening?"* she said. Jennifer's heart ached because she could not be there when her son needed her most. *"He is going to die while I am listening on the phone, and I am not going to be with him!"* Finally, just as Jennifer began to fear the very worst, the scene shifted.

After what seemed like hours, Cindie suddenly shouted, *"Oh my God, he's stopping!"* Seemingly shaken, yet relieved, she repeated herself. *"He's stopping!"* His little body had been seizing for more than ninety minutes, and finally, he stopped. Jennifer could hear his breathing ease, and she took a deep, reassuring breath herself. At that moment, she released the anxiety she had been so cautiously holding back and fell into a heap of emotion. The fear she had barely been able to contain turned into relieved gratitude. Her baby was going to be okay . . . this time.

There were no guarantees for Ethan's future, however, and daily life for the small family continued to remain very difficult. By the time Ethan was three years old, he had been seen by seven different neurologists and had failed eleven different medications prescribed to control the seizures. He underwent multiple EEGs and a multitude of additional tests. New drugs were added to the mix, and then replaced by others. All of the tests confirmed the abnormalities, but none of the medications successfully controlled the seizures.

Genetic testing was ordered after the family reached out to a specialist at UCLA. Some of the more common conditions that were known to trigger seizures were ruled out. Jennifer and Anthony thought the tests were complete. But they had skipped one test because the condition it confirmed was so rare. The test for Dravet Syndrome was left out but would prove to be critical in his diagnosis down the road. It was precisely the condition he had.

Ethan was three, and life was hard, but it certainly was not put on hold. Jennifer had Ethan with her all day, every day, and she did not stay sheltered at home. She refused to sit home and let life happen around her. It was easier to keep moving and try to live normally than to remain secluded.

Anthony's parents had been severely traumatized after almost losing their grandson while he was in their care. They no longer volunteered to take him overnight. Jennifer's parents had experienced an episode that landed them in an emergency room with their grandson as well. It was so frightening that they no longer felt qualified to watch him on their own either. Anthony was working as an ironworker and was out of the house most days. Jennifer's mom spent time helping with the shopping and would get them out of the house on occasion. But most of the time, Jennifer was left on her own.

She took Ethan everywhere with her. She was part of moms' groups and Bible studies. She put him in childcare at the church when she was in worship or Bible study. With him there, she could take a break with her church family and remain close enough to him if there was a problem. Jennifer went to scrapbook nights and hair appointments with him in tow. Wanting life to be typical for her little girl, she was the room mom in her daughter Eden's kindergarten class. Ethan didn't leave her side when she coordinated birthday and costume parties. She was driven by the desire for life to be as normal and complete as possible for her entire family.

Painfully though, everyday life for Ethan was far from ordinary. The continuous seizures had been torturous to his developing brain. He had autism and had suffered severe cognitive delays. The heartbreak and stress of it were overwhelming to his parents. There were no breaks, even for an occasional night out. They felt isolated, so they created their own village and support team. Their church family became very important because, with them, they could find solace.

# FALLING WHEN LIFE IS NOT FAIR

*"I don't want people to think that I didn't stumble or to feel like they aren't good enough because they think it was easy for me. That's not the journey that I had. As much as I am not proud of it, I had huge setbacks."*

### ~ Jennifer Fike

Newport Beach in California is quaint and beautifully peaceful. The mild weather and fresh ocean air make it a popular vacation destination for thousands of beachgoers. One of the moms in Jennifer's church group was among the masses who vacationed there every year by renting a house directly on the beach for the annual getaway. That particular year, she invited the small group of moms to come out with their kids to enjoy a day together playing and relaxing in the sun. Jennifer, excited to join in, packed Ethan's favorite snacks and toys to head out for an enjoyable day on the beach with friends. It was going to be fun for Ethan, she thought . . . until it wasn't.

The August weather was perfectly warm and sunny, accented by a light salty breeze. The moms were lined up in their beach chairs with their bare feet brushing the sand, excitedly chatting and leisurely sipping from their glasses of champagne. Directly in front of them, their children were giggling as they ran wildly toward the retreating water and then squealed as the surf chased them back again. They gleefully played together, splashing in the waves and building castles in the sand—everyone except Ethan.

Ethan was annoyed by the sand. He didn't like it sticking to his skin and his fingers and ultimately mixing into his snacks. He screamed and fussed at the challenge of keeping it off of him and out of his mouth. There was no interaction with the other children. He was completely oblivious to them and remained miserable in his own little world.

Jennifer took him to play in the water to see if he would like it. Not only did he love it, but he became obsessed with it. Many children with autism don't comprehend fear, and Ethan was determined to push the limits. He wanted to go out further than it was safe, and Jennifer was taxed with constantly pulling him closer to shore. But he fussed and screamed as if he were under siege when she attempted to control him. She finally took him away from the water and tried to distract him back on the beach by putting him on a blanket with his toys and some snacks. There were a few moments of silence, but he constantly turned his attention back to the water. That was not how she imagined the day would be. It was exhausting.

Jennifer was doing her best to put on a happy face and socialize with the other moms. But she wasn't having fun at all, and through her frustration, she began to drink more champagne. Jennifer knew that she was drinking much more than anyone else. Perhaps the other moms were feeling sorry for her and for the torment she was experiencing. Whatever the reason, no one challenged her excessive drinking. She wouldn't have cared if they had. She wasn't remotely concerned with what anyone thought. Her life was harder than anyone else there could ever imagine. She was justified in her over-consumption, she reasoned. The more Ethan complained, the more she attempted to escape with alcohol.

By the time she'd finally had enough, Jennifer realized that it was almost three in the afternoon. Anthony would be home from work soon, and she knew that he would be worried if she were not there when he arrived. It made her anxious to realize that, to get home, she needed to make her way through forty-five minutes of rush hour traffic. She began gathering her things to head home, but not without the scrutiny of a couple of the ladies. *"Are you okay to drive?"* one of them asked. Convincingly enough, she assured them that she would stop and grab something to eat just as soon as she reached Pacific Coast Highway. Everything would be fine, she reassured them. So then began the flawed and dangerous plan.

Jennifer grudgingly pushed Ethan and all of their belongings in the stroller to load everything into the SUV. She struggled to get the wet sandy child buckled into his car seat as he continued to fuss at her. It had been a frustrating day, and she was frantic to get them home before Anthony had a chance to miss them. She could do this, she thought. No, she needed to do this. But there was no denying that she was seriously impaired. In her haste and intoxicated state, she drove off, leaving the stroller behind in the street.

Once on the highway, she searched for the Dairy Queen to stick with her plan of finding something to eat. Indeed, that was all she needed. But taking her concentration off the route left her confused and heading in the wrong direction, so she pulled into a gas station to turn around. A bystander saw her pull into the station and recklessly maneuver a U-turn. He could see a child in the car, and by the way she was driving, he could also tell that she was not sober. He called 911.

Back on the highway and headed in the right direction, Jennifer continued on her dangerous trek home. The light she was approaching turned red just as her cell phone began ringing, and she looked down to see that it was Anthony. But glancing down for only a moment left her with little time to stop, causing her to hit the brakes hard. When she did, the cell phone flew off the seat onto the floor. She needed to answer and let him know that she was on her way home. She accelerated without realizing the next light had also turned red while she reached down to pick up the phone. There was no time to react. When she sat back up, she came to a screeching halt only because she plowed into the car that had stopped directly in front of her. The airbag went off, and it was over.

The police, who were already looking for her, pulled up behind the scene within moments. Barefoot and bikini-clad, Jennifer was put through a sobriety test in the middle of an upscale area of California's Pacific Coast Highway. There was no difficulty in concluding that she was way too impaired to be driving. It was fortunate that no one had been hurt in either car, but the consequences would still be extremely harsh. Not only did she have an accident while driving drunk, but she also had her small child in the car.

Jennifer thought she had reached rock bottom when she was sitting on the side of the road, handcuffed and unable to comfort her crying baby. He was anxiously reaching for her, and she could not hold him. She sobbed, and her heart ached for him. At that moment, Jennifer thought the experience would be like a light switch, and of course, she would stop drinking. But it wasn't that easy. She was painfully unaware of how she was using alcohol to help her cope with her grief and fear. She had not reached rock bottom yet.

Because she had received a DUI with Ethan in the car, her conviction was a felony. Jennifer's license was suspended, and she was sentenced to three years of probation. She was also ordered to complete a DUI first offender class, pay ten thousand dollars in restitution, and attend a MADD (Mothers Against Drunk Driving) panel. Her probation officer warned her that he would put her in jail if she were caught drinking while under his jurisdiction. She certainly wasn't going to drink and drive again.

A few months later, the Fikes invited another couple over for an evening visit. They hadn't seen these friends for a while so catching up was fun. As they casually drank, no one even considered Jennifer's probation. She didn't comprehend that there were restrictions for drinking at all. They socialized and drank well into the night, but nobody got drunk. Nobody in the group drank much at all. It didn't matter.

The following Saturday morning, Jennifer was due to attend her DUI first offender class. As she took her seat, she couldn't escape the pungent smell surrounding her. The entire room reeked of stale alcohol. There was no denying that some of her classmates, like her, had been drinking the night before.

The instructor started to enter the room and abruptly stopped at the door. He took a step back as if he'd run headfirst into an invisible barrier. He, of course, recognized the offensive stench and knew that some of the class had been drinking. His face became stern, and he continued walking into the room. He was livid that anyone would drink and then be bold enough to come to class. His eyes were piercing as he scanned the room and looked at the face of every individual. When he spoke, his voice was firm. *"Well, judging by the poor air quality we are experiencing in the room today, I think it would be a good day for a breathalyzer test on the entire class."* Jennifer was one of three to fail. She was suspended from class and told she would not be allowed back in until she received a court order clearing her to return.

Jennifer made a court appointment to see a judge and get reinstated into her class. She didn't understand that it was a big deal and thought it would just be a routine reinstatement—maybe a slap on the hand, but she wasn't sure. She had not driven herself to class the day of the breathalyzer and could prove it.

The judge looked up from her paperwork and addressed Jennifer in a stern tone. *"Mrs. Fike, have you seen your probation officer on this matter?"* Jennifer replied in a questioning tone because she wasn't sure why she would have. She definitely did not want to see him. *"No, Your Honor?"* She answered. The judge then instructed her to see her probation officer, adding that she would grant it if he approved her reinstatement. Suddenly, it was beginning to feel like the situation was more serious than she first understood.

Jennifer sat nervously in the probation officer's waiting area. Her head was spinning, and she wondered what kind of trouble she was in. When he finally called her into his office and sat her down, she could tell by his demeanor that things would not work out well for her.

*"What did I tell you I was going to do if you continued to drink?"* he asked firmly. She had that "oh crap" moment, realizing that things were, indeed, more serious than she'd understood them to

be. The next few minutes played out like a scene from a Hollywood movie. A female officer entered the office, put her against the wall, and handcuffed her to transport her to the county jail.

Jennifer was in the back of a police car, and her mind was racing. She still didn't comprehend just how much trouble she was facing. She wondered how long it would take to get through the process so she could be released. How mad was Anthony going to be? Would he be so angry that he wouldn't want her to come back home? He had to work; how would he take care of the kids if she wasn't allowed to get home quickly? Oh my God, her babies! She needed to be there to take care of them. She was overwhelmed with a crushing panic. She thought she had been at rock bottom when she was sitting handcuffed on a curb in Newport Beach. But what she was experiencing then was so much worse. It was impossible to feel more like a failure.

Getting processed into the system took the entire day. No one cared about the inmates or any amount of discomfort they were going through. They searched and then showered them, leaving them wet and cold while they took their time supplying them with the lightweight, used, and worn-out inmate garb. Then they were given a sheet and a small blanket. Pillows were not allowed. They were expected to sleep on a bunk equipped with a thin mat.

Entering the main population of the jail and beginning her life as a prisoner was terrifying. Jennifer had never been incarcerated, and she was reeling with the uncertainty of what the other inmates would be like. The stereotypes of what she'd seen in the movies left her imagination to run wild with thoughts of hardened, crazy women with a desire to dominate and intimidate her. Her expectations couldn't have been more wrong. What she saw in the other inmates was extreme sadness in a pool of severely broken people.

However, what was shocking and completely unexpected was the cruelty and verbal abuse that came from the deputies. Jennifer didn't have any experience being in jail, so she did everything wrong. There was a certain way to make your bed, address the deputies, and perform various other tasks that would invite their wrath if done incorrectly. Honestly, it didn't take much.

*"Fike!"* The deputy was within inches of her face. *"What a piece of shit you are! I bet your family is proud of you!"* she shouted sarcastically. Jennifer had never been spoken to like that, and she was mortified. But it was the way they were treated every day. No wonder they were all spiritually broken. That was the point Jennifer surmised. The staff did not want any problems from the inmates. So, they gained the upper hand, intimidated them, and worked to break their spirits right out of the starting gate. God forbid that any of the inmates shed any tears or showed any emotion. Jennifer was warned that such an emotional outbreak would be dealt with harshly. But she wanted to cry every minute of every one of those first several days. Those deputies had succeeded in breaking her along with everyone else.

If she were going to survive, she would keep to herself and go to AA meetings and church. She also worked in the kitchen to keep her mind occupied to avoid feeling sad. She read books and wrote letters as an outlet. When she was alone, she wept for her children and longed to be at home with Anthony.

## COMING TO TERMS

*"I had to learn to deal with my grief and fear because they were holding me hostage."*

### ~ Jennifer Fike

Even before going to jail, Jennifer had been attending AA meetings as required by her probation. It was there that she began to realize drinking was a coping mechanism—and a very poor one at that. There was a huge light bulb moment when she realized that drinking was a problem for her.

Now that there was uninterrupted time for her thoughts, she began to search her soul more deeply than ever. Then she had an epiphany. She realized that the reason she drank was that she was afraid. She was scared out of her mind! Nothing in her life's experience had prepared her to care for a seriously ill child. It terrified her to think that he could die in her care, and it would come unannounced, leaving her unable to forgive herself forever. She needed to find a more productive way to deal with her anxiety. She had always been interested in medicine. Nursing could give her the training she needed to overcome her fear. It was definitely an option.

*Well, here I am*, she thought, *sitting in jail in an AA meeting*. She had previously believed that she didn't belong here, surrounded by people with different types of addictions. It was an incredibly humbling moment when she realized that she *did* belong there. She wasn't any better than anyone else.

Every night in jail, she humbly prayed for one thing. *"Dear God, if it is your will, please let me go home and be with my children."* Anthony's family had taken over the household to help him out. His sister and her husband had moved in, and Jennifer was extremely grateful that they had given up a part of their lives to help Anthony. But she also questioned if Anthony would have her back. So, her prayer continued night after night. It was the only thing she asked for. It was the only thing she cared about.

God answered that prayer. Anthony had gone to see Jennifer's probation officer to plead his case. It wasn't for Jennifer's benefit, he told him. She needed to be at home to help care for their two children, one of which was severely disabled. He explained that he needed to work, and Jennifer's absence created serious difficulties for his family. Jennifer had been sentenced to 180 days. But the probation officer took pity on Anthony and his predicament and had her released after she'd completed forty-three days.

There were restrictions. Jennifer still didn't have a driver's license. She also had an ankle bracelet for house arrest and was only allowed to leave to get the children to school, grocery shop, go to church, and AA meetings. Several times a day she was required to breathe into a breathalyzer machine that reported the results directly to the authorities. There would be no cheating. She was so thankful to be at home that she didn't care. At that point, she just needed to concentrate on moving forward.

At home, Jennifer shook off the meek and fragile person the jail deputies had created. She was back, and she was as strong and determined as she had ever been. She was given another chance, and this time she would be sure there was no alcohol in the house! What if her probation officer paid a surprise visit? She was not going back to jail.

Jennifer served the balance of her time on house arrest. Since she still didn't have a driver's license, she bought a bicycle and a small trailer to pull her kids behind her to get them to school every day. Her mom took her grocery shopping, and Anthony took the family to church every Sunday. The church family had remained very important to them. Jennifer had been in Bible study for years, so she had already built the foundation for those critical relationships. But then, more than ever, she needed the strength and hopefulness that the church family fostered. They became so involved that they were also co-leaders of several Bible study groups and spent four to five days a week in various gatherings and activities.

Through prayer, church services, and AA meetings, she began to heal. There was a lot of self-reflection. The way she had been living was not who she was. It would not allow her to be there for her children if she didn't get her act together. The idea of studying nursing that had first occurred to her while she had in jail continued to be at the forefront of her thoughts. She couldn't help her son in her current state, and he deserved her best. Both of her children did. Jennifer knew that she needed to become a nurse. She didn't want to feel afraid anymore. Besides, she knew Ethan would need a nurse forever, and it might as well be her. It was precisely how she could empower herself and take back control.

A week after Jennifer completed her four months of house arrest, she enrolled in school to study nursing. People in AA had warned her not to try and do everything at once. But Jennifer needed things to start falling into their proper place. She needed to find normalcy sooner rather than later. Anthony needed to find his escape in Jujitsu, for her kids to be in school, and the family regularly attending church. Her goal was to work towards something bigger and better, so she started school.

Jennifer still did not have a driver's license, but she had great friends who helped her out. In the beginning, her friend, Erica, sat in the car with Ethan while Jennifer took her assessment test at Riverside Community College. Erica and her husband Kevin helped a lot by getting her to classes and anywhere else she needed to be. *Thank God for them!* she thought. There were others too. It was as if God was putting the people she needed in the right places at just the right times. It was confirmation that she had made the correct decision.

The first year in school was tough. Studying and completing assignments was a challenge all on its own. Sometimes the only time to study came late at night or early in the morning when everyone else was asleep. She had a family and a household to take care of, and Ethan was still having seizures once a month or so. But the timing was not a given. The seizures could still not be predicted.

## TESTED AGAIN

*"Sometimes we are tested.*
*Not to show our weaknesses,*
*but to discover our strengths."*

**~ Goubert Botha**

Jennifer was beyond exhausted. Her body ached, and her limbs felt heavy. She had been awake for hours after staying up late the night before writing a paper. The early morning was filled with more study and the balance of the day dedicated to necessary household chores. She just wanted to be finished for the day. It was beginning to get dark, and she longed to get Ethan to sleep and pour her own worn-out body into bed. There were just a few more things to get done.

Anthony was at Jujitsu, and Eden was with Gramma for the night. Ethan was playing contently on the floor. Jennifer was busy working around him when she looked down to see him going into a seizure. She dropped what she was doing and scooped him up to place him on his side on the bed.

It would seem that the scenario should be routine. But every episode was unique and frightening. Most of the seizures were shorter in duration, but some still lasted longer than usual.

In Bible study, many intense conversations had occurred among the group about surrendering to God when it involved their children. Everyone agreed that every situation needed to be handed over to God.

But when the conversation circled around their children, the conflict was in the belief that it was the Lord's child versus it was my child. Jennifer had said, *"No, this is my child."* She was afraid that she would be sacrificing him by surrendering him, and that fear, in turn, caused doubt.

Even though she had grown up Christian and had been a devout believer, she was angry with God for not giving her a healthy son. Why had God done this to Ethan? Jennifer and Anthony struggled intensely with the cards they were dealt, and both questioned, *"God, how could you?"*

It had become a tradition for the Bible study group to watch *The Passion of the Christ* every year on Good Friday. Jennifer emotionally watched with the others as Christ carried his cross, and Mary reflected on memories of him as a child. Of course, any parent would feel the pain and suffering of their child. But Jennifer knew that he was created for that moment. She knew that her son had not been born to be sacrificed for the greater good. *I am too selfish*, she thought. *I could never let him suffer if there was a way that I could prevent it.*

Ethan continued to seize on the bed while Jennifer waited it out. The prolonged seizures didn't happen as much anymore, so that one was out of the ordinary. After twenty minutes, she could hear him having difficulty breathing. Jennifer tried to soothingly coax him as he continued to convulse. She had the suction machine and all of the necessary tools to help him through, so he wasn't in immediate distress. But she started to dial 911, pausing before completing the call to wait to see if things took a turn for the worse. *It's going to stop, and then I will have called them out here for nothing*, she thought. But it wasn't stopping, and twenty minutes soon turned into thirty. Jennifer was exhausted. But the heaviness in her body left her feeling beyond tired. She felt desperate. She thought that this must be what God wanted.

As the seizure approached forty minutes, she felt helpless, and not in her most gracious voice; she began to pray. *"Fine God! If this is your child, and he is truly not mine, then just take him,"* she cried. *"Just take him so that this will stop."* She pleaded. *"He can't keep doing this. If this is your child and not mine, then just take him home. Just let it stop."* Perhaps her prayer was not superficial for the first time and came wholly from her heart as she completely surrendered her son. She said her prayer, and in her brokenness, completely gave him to God.

What happened next was a miracle. In the very instant that she completed that prayer, the seizure stopped. It was so immediate that it could not have been anything but God's hand. Relief swept over her, and she felt like she had not been forsaken or forgotten. Jennifer knew that God heard her prayer at that moment, but she also realized that the episode had not been about Ethan. It was about her.

# SCHOOL

*"A difficult time can be more readily endured
if we retain the conviction that our existence holds a purpose—
a cause to pursue, a person to love, a goal to achieve."*

### ~ John Maxwell

In the beginning, Jennifer only took one online class. She needed to know if she could manage the schedule on top of what she was already doing. But she took it in a condensed format, which brought it down from a sixteen-week course to an eight-week course. That way, she could take two courses back-to-back and complete two in sixteen weeks instead of just one. She tested her theory in the first semester to see if she could manage the additional workload. She was able to get A's in those classes, confirming that she could do it.

By then, Ethan was seizure-free for about thirty days at a time. His parents wanted more for him, but their frustrated doctor told them the seizures would never be completely controlled. *"This is as good as it's going to get,"* he said. His tone was harsh. He said they needed to be satisfied with things as they were and be grateful that they were not worse. But living with things as they were meant living with the possibility of breakthrough seizures every day. Jennifer and Anthony were livid at his lack of commitment. What kind of doctor would just give up?

The family simply wasn't going to settle for that. Anthony's sister, Lisa, was in medical school, and his mom, Cindie, was working on her doctorate. They had strong connections in the medical field and began searching throughout the country for the best specialists. There were two. One was at Johns Hopkins in Baltimore, and one at Sutter Health in Sacramento. Because traveling with Ethan was such an issue, they chose the closer neurologist in Sacramento.

The doctor had become world-renowned for his ability to control seizure episodes for months at a time. Ethan was then five years old, and his seizures had created severe developmental delays and caused secondary autism. The doctor stated that he'd wished that he could have started treating Ethan when he was two years old instead of five. He may have been able to stop some of the damage. As it was, he was able to get the seizures under control so that they became a rarity instead of an everyday occurrence. The doctor's care for Ethan had made an enormous impact that was felt by the entire family.

Jennifer still attempted to take the bulk of her classes online, and she was able to complete most of her general education requirements that way. But juggling school and home responsibilities was every bit the challenge she knew it would be. It took a ton of organization. In the beginning, she would work on school every night from eight o'clock to midnight after getting the kids to bed. So, her priorities after her family became school and church.

By the time Ethan started kindergarten and Eden was in the second grade, Jennifer could attend the classes on campus that weren't available online. Since Ethan's seizures were under control, it was safe to venture out for a few hours each day.

Meanwhile, Eden was a perfectly healthy seven-year-old child that did all of the things healthy children do. They had her in ballet and tap; she played soccer and took piano lessons. Jennifer would be on the sidelines watching her games while making flashcards or with her cell phone studying for an exam. She could also use the time to study while Eden was taking piano lessons.

Anthony started to heal gradually too, and the two of them became a well-organized team. They had to work hard, but they were committed to each other and their children. Anthony was supportive of Jennifer's goal and took charge of things around the house often so she could sit at a Denny's or Starbucks for a few hours at a time to study.

Jennifer received her associate degree in four years instead of two because of all of her challenges. Then she had to continue for another year at the junior college to complete her nursing prerequisites. Never did she allow herself to be discouraged at the amount of time it took. There were some challenging days, when she felt the weight of exhaustion. But in the long run, she chose to be grateful for the opportunity and the ability to push on. She had to for Ethan.

# JUDGEMENT DAY

*"So rarely do you get an opportunity*
*to redefine the person that you are*
*and ditch the baggage."*

### ~ Jennifer Fike

Jennifer already knew that she would have to jump through hoops to get accepted into nursing school. Nursing is considered to be the most ethical of professions. It wasn't the DUI that was going to present the problem. Jennifer had Ethan in the car with her, and that made her conviction a felony.

She had completed her DUI classes, attended her AA meetings, and sat before the MADD panel as required. After she met those requirements, she was allowed to petition the courts to reduce her conviction from a felony to a misdemeanor. There were no guarantees. But in a leap of faith, she had already completed the studies required to apply to nursing school. She prayed that it was not all for nothing.

Jennifer spent hours gathering documentation to present to the judge. She had character reference letters from Eden's teachers, Ethan's doctor, her Bible study leader, and more from her professors, personal friends, and family. She took those and her school transcripts to court, hoping that she had built a good case to have her charges reduced.

In the waiting area, Jennifer sat with several others in various predicaments, all with their own desired outcomes for their cases. In casual conversation, she began to develop quite a cheering squad. *God only knows what these people are in here for*, she thought. Looking at them, she felt grateful to have their support. She sat anxiously awaiting her turn in the hot seat, hoping that the enthusiasm of her dubious tribe would be shared by the judge reviewing her case.

The bailiff had not collected her documents when they called on her. So, the judge began to question her sternly. *"Mrs. Fike, is there any reason I should consider your case? Do you have any supporting documents for me to review?"* Jennifer readily responded, *"Yes, Your Honor, I do."* The judge instructed the bailiff to bring her the overstuffed folder and announced that she would take a short recess to review Jennifer's papers.

Jennifer felt sick to her stomach. She was terrified. Her entire future and all she had worked so hard for was on the line. Her ragtag posse continued to encourage her with absolute surety that she would be granted a reduction of her charges. Still, she did not want to be overconfident, only to then experience defeat. It had been such an arduous journey, and so much depended on the judge's decision. If it didn't happen, it didn't matter how hard she had worked to get all A's or how she'd aced the entrance exam for nursing school. It was the only thing left standing in the way of possible acceptance into a nursing program, and it was huge.

When the judge came back into the courtroom, you could hear a pin drop. The air was thick with anticipation. All who were in the room had become invested in the decision at this point. Jennifer held her breath and attempted to camouflage the nervous shaking of her hands. The silence was finally broken as the judge began to address Jennifer directly. *"Mrs. Fike,"* she started, *"I have to tell you that in my entire career, it is difficult to recall anyone who has done such a one-eighty in their life. Your supporting documents are impressive, and it is clear that you have worked very hard and have developed a huge support group."* Jennifer let out the breath she had been unaware she was holding and began feeling more hopeful. The judge continued, *"It is my privilege to reduce your charges, and I wish you well."* Then she turned her attention, *"Bailiff, could you please get Mrs. Fike her documents and let her get out of here!"* The entire courtroom erupted in applause and cheers. Jennifer was overwhelmed with gratitude. When she reached her car, she clutched the steering wheel and paused for a moment to thank God.

## NURSING SCHOOL AND PASSING THE BOARDS

*"The last moment of feeling powerless was gone, and I was finally in charge of my own destiny."*

### ~ Jennifer Fike

Every day that Jennifer was allowed to be in nursing school was a gift. But it certainly was not going to be a cakewalk.

When Jennifer attended nursing school, she was only pulled out of class once because Ethan was having a seizure. But Ethan's care while Jennifer was in school was still a challenge. Online classes were no longer an option. She was required to be on campus full-time for her classes. She recruited people like Eden's teachers, her classmates, and other moms, including the Bible study moms who all donated their time so that Jennifer could continue school. Anthony's dad, Pat, retired and started watching Ethan and taking him to his therapy most days. His contribution was amazing, and he became the family hero. Still, managing the different shifts of Ethan's care was almost a full-time job. But Jennifer was determined to push on.

Jennifer was stressed out much of the time, though. When she was home, she was thinking about school. When at school, she felt guilty about not being home. Mostly, she was afraid for Ethan and worried that he was with someone who didn't understand and know him as she did. She was conflicted—while she was studying for him, she also sacrificed her time with him. She knew that the big picture was going to be more beneficial for him, though. The other thing that plagued her was that she was robbed of time with her perfectly healthy daughter. She was missing so much of Eden's childhood.

Even when she was home, a lot of her time needed to be dedicated to studying. There continued to be late nights and early morning hours spent on the effort. The work was hard, and the time requirements left her exhausted. Time passed slowly, and the demands between home and school were tough.

The time that elapsed from her first day at junior college had been seven years. The additional responsibilities added years to the average timeline. Jennifer was never discouraged and was grateful that she had even been given the opportunity. Through her hardships, she remained committed and driven. She could never have accepted giving in to the difficulties by letting even one of her responsibilities slip. Her grades were exceptional.

After years of hard work and incredible perseverance, Jennifer earned her BSN and graduated with honors in December 2016.

Believe it or not, she still had one more mountain to climb, and it was a big one. The petition to take her state boards to become a registered nurse would be her final challenge, and there were no guarantees. She had come so far by completing her studies. She had even done a lot of the leg work by getting her charges reduced and her records expunged. She needed to appeal to the state to prove that she was worthy of becoming a nurse.

Jennifer was required to provide all of the paperwork she needed to be accepted into nursing school, including the court records. In addition, she needed more reference letters, the police report, and a letter she wrote on her own behalf. She needed to plead the case and explain why the state should trust her and accept her to such a position. She provided all of the required paperwork. Then all she could do was wait to see if the state would approve a test date for her.

Weeks passed. All of Jennifer's classmates had received their test dates, and many had taken them and passed. Jennifer checked her email multiple times a day. She felt more anxious with every passing day. But she continued to have faith in God that things would work out. All she could do was pray; otherwise, she had no control.

Jennifer had applied to the state in December after she graduated, and it was now the end of February. She and Anthony had saved for months to put a new pool in the backyard of their Southern California home to get Ethan some much-needed exercise. He loved to swim, and they had been forced to take him to Anthony's parents' house or a friend's house to get him into a pool. It was going to be so much more convenient, and he would be able to swim more often.

The couple was relaxing by the pool with some friends one evening. Perhaps out of habit, Jennifer reached for her phone, and while she had it in her hand, she checked her emails. There it was: the email she had been so anxiously awaiting was sitting in her inbox. The color left her face, and as she turned pale, her expression froze. She gasped, stopping the conversation that had been carrying on around her. Anthony was focused on her and knew what was going on from her expression. She looked as if she'd seen a ghost. *"The email from the state is there, isn't it?"* he said. *"Yes,"* she replied. *"But I am terrified to open it."* Anthony and her friend excitedly pushed her. *"Open it!"* they shrieked in unison.

The minute Jennifer clicked on the email and saw what was inside, she dropped to her knees. She couldn't stop the tears. It was the first time since she'd started the journey that she had allowed herself to unveil her feelings. They rushed over her uncontrollably. It was finally the end, and the emotion she felt was profound.

Everyone was screaming and jumping around in excitement. Anthony had to hold Jennifer up to keep her knees from buckling under her overwhelming relief. It had been such a long battle— longer than she had ever imagined it would be, but worth every minute of the fight.

Jennifer took her state boards to become a registered nurse on April 13th. It was exactly eight years to the day of being released from jail. Of course, she passed. It was important to turn that day into a lucky day. And it was.

## TIME TO GO TO WORK

*"There is proof that God has a sense of humor.*
*Without knowing anything about me personally,*
*the hospital assigned me to the neurological unit."*

### ~ Jennifer Fike

Jennifer had searched for local hospitals and sent resumes to all of them. San Antonio Regional Hospital was the first to reach out to her. She was familiar with them because she knew someone who had their baby there. Otherwise, she knew little about them.

Her interview was scheduled for 8:00 a.m. She liked to be the first because she felt it was the best strategy to make the best and more lasting impression. The first person she met with was the director, who was extremely personable and easy to be around. Jennifer's equally big personality meshed with hers immediately, and she found the director to be both fun and funny. The director walked her around the facility while talking to her like she was already hired. Jennifer was already confident in the way she was able to relate to people. She wasn't shy, but at the age of thirty-eight she had life experience that the younger applicants could not compete with. After the tour, they went to her office for the questions and an actual interview.

Suddenly, one of the staff managers burst through the door unannounced. She began to speak to the director immediately and then realized that she wasn't alone. *"Oh!"* she said. *"You are interviewing."* Then the two of them continued to interact. Jennifer laughed out loud at the scene, thinking they were more like a comedy team than colleagues in a hospital. She was wholly amused and delighted. She thought, *Oh yes, I am absolutely going to work here!* If these two comic relief personalities are in charge, she thought, *I definitely want in.* They liked her too. Before she reached her car, they called her to schedule a second interview with a panel of eight people consisting of the educators and charge nurses. She needed to get past the scrutiny of those who would be her peers.

The interview was scheduled for two weeks out. Meanwhile, Jennifer had done some research on her resume and realized just how outdated it was. It was critical to make a good impression on this group, or if need be, any future interviewers she might come into contact with. She knew she already had the required skills for the job; now, she needed to work on her professional presentation. She found a great resume template online with an EKG strip across the top. It looked completely specialized and fitting for a medical professional. She filled in her details on that template and updated her information. Jennifer then took her finished document to an office supply store and had multiple copies printed onto high-quality paper stock. After bundling them in individual packets along with her letters of recommendation for each of the interviewers, she felt confidently prepared and ready for them.

Once again, Jennifer had scheduled her interview so that she would be first on the schedule. On her way to the meeting, she stopped and bought bagels and cream cheese. Arriving about ten minutes early, she went directly into the conference room where most of the attendees were already gathered. She introduced herself, and one of them, with a look of surprise, kindly told her, *"Oh, we are not quite ready for you yet."* Jennifer answered back, *"That's okay; I knew I was first on your calendar today. Since it's early, I thought you may not have had time yet to have breakfast."* Then she placed her goods in the middle of the table and proceeded back to the waiting area.

Ten minutes passed when one of the educators came to get her from the lobby. Jennifer could not help but smile when she noticed just a hint of cream cheese on her lip. She knew then that they had indulged in the breakfast she'd brought them.

Jennifer felt at ease with the panel in front of her. She had already gotten a sense of how the group interacted by her initial experience with the casual and lighthearted dispositions of the director and manager on her first visit. Her caring and cheery personality meshed perfectly with this group. They didn't go particularly easy on her, however. Their questions were pointed and designed to determine her knowledge and level of grit. At the same time, her big personality was out there for all to see.

Toward the end of the questioning, the panel asked Jennifer why they should consider her over any of the other equally qualified candidates. *"First, I will never leave to go work for the biggest medical group in the area because I don't like them. Second, I am thirty-eight years old and am finished having babies. You will never lose me to maternity leave. Finally,"* she continued, *"I will outwork any other candidate you are considering."*

When the interview was finished, Jennifer thanked them and told them, *"I sincerely hope you have a lot of great candidates."* Then she concluded by adding, *"But none as good as me."* Everyone laughed, and Jennifer departed with a good feeling. It was a feeling that was well calculated. As it turns out, the panel genuinely liked her and called that afternoon to offer her a position at their hospital.

It was the responsibility of the charge nurses to select the unit where the candidate would fit best. Jennifer had not mentioned that she had an epileptic son. Without knowing her history or how she'd gotten there, they placed her on the hospital's neurological unit. Coincidence? Jennifer says that it's proof God has a sense of humor—he indeed had a say. Of course, it was a perfect fit.

A couple of years had passed when Loma Linda University School of Nursing , Jennifer's alma mater, expressed a need for RNs to help teach new nursing students. Jennifer had become friends with most of the staff and had maintained contact with them. One of the staff members, who was also a mentor and Jennifer's most influential instructor, had posted on social media that the university needed RNs to teach. That mentor, Brandie, was so excited to hear from Jennifer and said, *"You are perfect! When can you come in?"*

She entered the classroom where the interview was to occur only to find a person who had been an instructor of hers for years. It was both surreal and had the feel of home. In the halls, she passed several more of her past instructors, all of whom wanted to know if she would return to them to teach. *"That's the rumor,"* she said.

Then, the dean came into the room and gave Jennifer a big hug. She said, *"Well, if you are interviewing Fike, it's a yes from me because she is one of my own."* That seemed to set the tone for what was supposed to be an interview. Instead of answering questions, she was instructed on what she would be doing. There was no interviewing going on at all. She was told where to get fit for her lab coat, and that was the beginning. When she arrived back home, she received an email telling her she'd been hired.

As of this writing, Jennifer still works full-time as an RN where she first started at San Antonio Regional Hospital. She also teaches part-time at Loma Linda University School of Nursing. *"Bedside nursing is my passion. I could never see giving it up,"* Jennifer said, and then added, *"I also didn't know that I would love teaching, but I do."*

## YOUR GAME PLAN:

If you are parenting a child with disabilities, as with any other challenge, it can be helpful to connect with others in your exact situation.

- One of the best books I have read on parenting an autistic child is *Welcome to My Life: A Personal Journey Through Autism*, by Laurie L Hellmann. The author tells the story of how her family copes with daily life and how she came to terms with her role. She also emphasizes the importance of being involved with a community of people in the same circumstances, offering support to one another. In the book, Hellmann notes, *"This is my life, and it's beautiful beyond anything I could have ever dreamed."*

What drives your passion? Determine your "why." Uncovering what motivates you and focusing on that purpose will help you get beyond the most difficult challenges in your life.

- Do some soul searching on this point. For help, I suggest you read Mike McCallister's book, *Unlock the Power of Why*. He quotes John C Maxwell, who said, *"Find your WHY, and you'll find your WAY."*

Author and inspirational speaker, Simon Senek, has said, *"It is only when you understand your "why" (or your purpose) that you'll be more capable of pursuing the things that give you fulfillment. It will serve as your point of reference for all your actions and decisions from this moment on, allowing you to measure your progress and know when you have met your goal."*

- What are your goals for you or your family? Who is in your circle of influence to help you and answer questions? Research the groups who share your needs. Ask for help from others on this step if you need it.

(Read the "Winning Points" below, then re-visit this exercise for any additions that the review of that section may prompt.)

## WINNING POINTS:

I asked Jennifer who benefits most from her sharing her story. She told me her story was for anybody who was going through something they feel is insurmountable—people dealing with grief or some sort of loss. *"I couldn't have dealt with anything else without first dealing with my grief because it was my grief that held me hostage. I have a special place in my heart for parents of special needs children and anyone dealing with addiction. I would like especially to reach out to them."*

In full disclosure, Jennifer is my daughter. This particular chapter was both heartfelt and very difficult to write. I was on the frontlines when this story unfolded and understood the despair and challenge of what she experienced. But I also had the joy of witnessing her overcoming. I could not be prouder of what she has accomplished. My grandson, Ethan, is fifteen as of this writing. He is a precious being that could not have been gifted with more fitting parents. They have not been perfect, but they are perfect for him.

On a side note to my granddaughter, Eden, who is now a certified medical assistant after graduating from high school a year early—

You weathered the storm, and because your parents were so great, you didn't always know you were in the midst of one. You have been a champion, a great sister, and an advocate for your brother. You are the light of my life!

## STEPS THAT JENNIFER TOOK WHEN FEELING OVERWHELMED BY HER CIRCUMSTANCES

- **Build a support system:** Jennifer and Anthony became more involved with their church. They also had a circle of friends and family to help support them. But none of that happened in the beginning. They set out with a purpose to find the help and support they needed.

- **Focus on "wins" and things you can control to improve your situation:** This includes coming to terms with the things you can't control. Focusing on even the smallest wins can make your day brighter.

- **Be proactive about change:** In other words, don't wait for things to happen around you. It's always okay to ask for help. Reaching out to support groups and friends can be beneficial. Whether on your own or with assistance, seek out ways to help make your everyday life easier.

- **Know your strengths and take power:** Jennifer is a super organizer and is great at building relationships. She has been a great advocate for Ethan and has been able to get him into many of the programs he needs for his development. Again, seek help if you need it.

- **Be kind to yourself, and do things that make you happy:**
  Make a list of the things that make you happy, regardless
  of how small. Make it a fun list! If you are a reader, runner,
  baker, gardener, golfer . . . include whatever pleases you.
  Make a little time for yourself every day.

## OVERCOMING EMOTIONS

*(those that come with being the parent of a special needs child)*

One of the best books I've read deals directly with the emotional
strain plaguing special needs parents is *Spectrum Secrets* by Sharline
Mashack.

In her book, she addresses all of the following, with examples:

- Shock and Disbelief

- Anger

- Guilt

- Fear and Panic

- Embarrassment

- Shame

- Resentment

- Sadness and Grief

- Worry and Anxiety

- Loneliness, Betrayal, Exhaustion

The author offers steps to build emotional toughness. She also
talks about what your child might be experiencing and how to deal
with common things like wandering, tuning out, and meltdowns.

The book is an exceptional read full of true stories about the
struggles of real special needs parents.

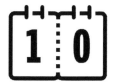

## FINAL SCORE:

If you would like to contact Jennifer to speak to outreach groups for special needs children or those facing addiction, you can email her at fikusmaximus@hotmail.com.

Jennifer's recommended reading: Eckhart Toll – *The Power Of Now: A Guide to Spiritual Enlightenment.*

**Groups that can help with Epilepsy and Autism:**

Epilepsy support groups: www.epilepsy.com

Autism Speaks: www.autismspeaks.org

# JASON KOGER

# CHAPTER SIX

---

# THE FAITH
# OF A CHAMPION

*"To trust God in the light is nothing,
but to trust him in the dark – That is faith."*

~ **C.H. Spurgeon**

# JASON AND JENNY KOGER'S STORY

For weeks Jason had been working almost nonstop at his dad's construction company. The hours were so extreme that he felt like he had been working around the clock. The plumbing contractor's business had taken off, and it seemed that there was no catching up to the work demand. It was Friday afternoon, and after a long week, he was tired!

Jason's wife, Jenny, was busy herself holding down a full-time job as a promotions' coordinator. On that afternoon, much like every other, after working at that demanding job, she came home to care for their two young children, ages twenty-one months and three months. After arriving home, Jason began helping Jenny with some errands around the house. It was a typical Friday afternoon, but it was the last one that would feel normal for a while.

On that following Saturday, the house was buzzing with more activity than normal. Jenny's brother was getting married, and her soon-to-be sister-in-law had stopped by to talk about the upcoming wedding. Jenny was at her computer helping with the design of their wedding invitations.

It was early March, and Mother Nature had gifted Owensboro, Kentucky, with the first sunny day of the season. Jason stepped outside to take a moment to himself, squinting as the warm rays of the sun touched his face. He casually picked up a basketball and sank a couple of shots, and began thinking he could use some quiet time in the fresh Kentucky air. He checked in with Jenny and set out on his four-wheel ATV to take a short ride.

Jason had lived on the property all of his life. He purchased the house from his dad when Jenny became pregnant with their second daughter. His cousin Travis and uncle Mike lived in two of the five houses on the farm. All of those properties were occupied by family members and had been in the family for years. It was always the plan that he and his cousins would remain there to raise their children the same way they were raised. So Jason was very familiar with the lay of the land and had planned to be gone five to ten minutes at the most.

It was late afternoon, but the sun was still shining bright on the familiar path in front of him. He was moving at a slow, relaxing pace, taking his time in the peaceful setting. He had taken this ride thousands of times before, yet the beauty of his surroundings did not escape him. The air was crisp, and the freshness of it filled his lungs. The blue-sky hovered overhead, its rich hues broken up by a few patches of cotton-white clouds. In the distance, he could see the sun beating down on an empty cornfield. Soon, it would be blanketed by new green vegetation, and later it would be filled with tall golden stalks. His focus took him far beyond his path, leaving him clueless to the danger looming directly in front of him. He started to ride over a culvert that he'd been over so many times that crossing it was routine. That time, however, as he rode over, he felt an unexpected thump just above his rib cage that made him suddenly break and come to an immediate stop.

Jason didn't see the downed power line until it was resting square in the middle of his chest. He looked down, stunned at the discovery, and was then in disbelief that it hadn't shocked him. *It must not be hot*, he surmised. But no sooner had that thought passed when it suddenly hit him hard with 7200 volts of electricity (an electric chair only uses 6900 volts). The intensity of the shock pulsed through his entire body.

For the brief moment before blacking out, he could hear the sound of a strange vibration and felt it surging through his bones. It forced the grinding of his teeth. Its grip held him captive for the next thirty seconds, eventually stopping his heart and savagely convulsing his unconscious body. Then, as suddenly as it started, it stopped. When it released him, he was tossed to the ground like a rag doll, and his right shoe shot out thirty feet from the strength of electricity exiting his body. Fortunately, the force of his landing started his heart again and brought him back to consciousness.

As soon as he could see daylight again, he began to sense an intense and excruciating burning pain. He felt like his insides were on fire. In fact, that is how electricity burns—from the inside out. His immediate thought was that he needed to immerse himself in the water of a nearby ditch to put out the fire and relieve the scorching agony. The urgency to get there took over his entire being.

Jason's cousin, Travis, had seen what was happening from his property a short distance away and rushed to the scene on his ATV. In disbelief, he watched what looked like fireworks consuming the entirety of Jason's body. Shaking and in near panic, he rushed to Jason's side but was not at all certain that he would find his cousin alive. When Jason began to stand up, his cousin was astonished. Jason was confused and speaking gibberish about the need to get to the nearby trench to put out the consuming fire. Travis knew he could not allow him to enter the ditch. He could see that Jason was covered with open wounds and understood that the rancid water could cause a serious infection. So he grabbed ahold of him and began to pull him away from the ditch.

Once he had him restrained, Travis called 911 and his dad Mike—Jason's uncle. Next, he called Jason's parents. He didn't call Jenny first because he was afraid that Jason would not survive and did not want to be the one to tell her. Nobody wanted that job. Jason's parents called his sister, Holly, who finally alerted Jenny that her husband had been in a terrible accident. Mike was on the scene within minutes. He cradled Jason in his lap and waited for the emergency vehicles to arrive with the desperately needed help. Jason was reeling with thoughts of disbelief that he was alive, and he believed that he was, by some miracle, okay.

But there were visible injuries. There was an imprint of a checkmark on Jason's right foot from the pedal where he was burned through his shoe while he was pushing on the brake. His left thumb was hanging by a mere thread of skin, and his fingers were curled and frozen like a claw except for his middle finger, which was stuck straight up. His right arm was inflamed in an angry shade of red and covered with large raised white blisters indicating third-degree burns. In between his middle finger and his ring finger, there was a hole the size of a pencil eraser where electricity exited his body leaving behind a destructive fury. In reality, his injuries were much more serious than they appeared. No one would understand to what extent until they reached the hospital in Nashville hours later.

Jenny had been working on the computer designing wedding invitations and was frustrated when the power suddenly went out. The electric shock to Jason's body had shut off the power to the entire neighborhood. She looked up from her work and had no sooner stood up to investigate when the power came back on, and the phone rang. The call was from Jason's sister, Holly, and the news was startling. *"Accident where?"* Jenny asked frantically. But Holly wasn't certain. She only knew that Jason had been in an accident somewhere on the vast property. She told Jenny in fragmented sentences that he was hurt—that he had been *"hit."*

Jenny's immediate thought was that he must have been struck by a car. But that didn't make sense because she knew that he was riding on the property, not the road. Still, she dropped the phone as if it had suddenly become hot enough to burn her and desperately ran outside to see if she could find Jason, but he was nowhere in sight.

A neighbor across the street noticed Jenny anxiously searching the street and ran to her to see what was wrong. Jenny was visibly shaken, and her voice trembled as she told him that Jason had been in an accident somewhere on the farm on his four-wheeler. She was in a near panic because she didn't know where. Suddenly, the sound of sirens began blasting in the distance. Her eyes started to fill as the terror of what might be happening began to overpower her thoughts. She needed to locate him now! *"How can I help?"* her neighbor pleaded. *"Please drive me to find him,"* she cried. Jason's truck was parked with the keys still in it, and the two of them jumped in it and set out to search.

Jenny arrived at the accident just before the emergency vehicles got there. When she reached Jason, he seemed surprisingly alert, and seeing her in such distress, he tried to calm her fears. He told her that he was fine and thought he was only going to lose his thumb. *"See,"* he reassured her. *"It's not so bad."*

When the ambulance arrived, the EMTs knew immediately that they were dealing with a serious injury. They rushed to load him into the vehicle and worked to keep him stable en route to the hospital. Jenny sat in the front next to the driver and listened as Jason anxiously rambled. He was speaking clearly, though, and seemed so alert that she was convinced that his injuries were not all that serious.

Jason continued to talk to her nonstop from the back to assure her he was fine. He recalled that his recently deceased grandfather had been a single-arm amputee and told the story to comfort Jenny further. *"Papa lost his whole arm. I am only going to lose my thumb,"* he told her, convinced that was the extent of his injuries. Obviously in shock, he repeated it over and over. Jenny was unsure of whether he was trying to convince her or himself.

Up to that moment, Jenny surmised that Jason had gotten into an accident on his ATV. But then the EMT who was driving tried to prepare her for what was coming. He told her that as an electrical shock victim, Jason would be transferred to a better-equipped hospital to treat his burns. Jenny's attention abruptly shot toward him. *"What are you talking about?"* she said, shaken by what she'd just heard. It was the first time she became aware of what had happened to Jason, and for the first time, she feared that his injuries might be more serious than she first thought.

The atmosphere was frantic at the hospital in Owensboro. The medical staff urgently rushed in and out of the room in a frenzy as they determined the best way to treat Jason's injuries. Jenny felt invisible as the activity rushed around her. In the distance, she overheard a doctor shout orders at the staff. *"We need to get this kid out of here now, or he is going to lose his arms!"* Jenny was in disbelief. *Surely, God would not allow such a thing,* she thought and chose to believe it was conjecture.

Finally, one of the staff stopped at Jason's bedside and informed him that he needed to be rushed to a burn unit. Jenny had already been prepared for that news by the ambulance driver. But they still waited for what seemed like an eternity.

Finally, Jason was put on a helicopter and airlifted to Vanderbilt Hospital in Nashville. Jenny stayed behind to sign consent paperwork and planned to make the drive following Jason's parents within an hour.

Once the helicopter was in the air, Jason looked down over his left shoulder and was able to see the flashing lights of the emergency vehicles still on his property below. It was surreal.

The EMT on the helicopter told him that she needed to insert a catheter, and he nodded, giving his consent. He didn't understand what he saw at the time, but the liquid filling the bag more closely resembled the color of maple syrup than urine. His kidneys were fighting hard to remove the toxins from his body caused by internal injuries. During the helicopter ride, he was not given any medication for the pain for fear that his kidneys could not handle the additional stress. The immediate concern was that his kidneys could be overwhelmed and shut down. In that scenario, the battle for his life would be lost.

After arriving at the hospital in Nashville, Jason was placed on a steel table in an otherwise cold and empty room. It was so frigid there that for a fleeting moment, Jason thought he was in a morgue and wondered if he was dead or dying. But a technician reassured him that it was a sterile room called a hydro room where burn victims were treated with a pressure washer to remove dead or dying skin after a severe burn. It wasn't clear if he'd receive medication for what he was told would be an uncomfortable procedure. Fortunately, afterward, Jason didn't recall going through it. When that process was completed, he was prepped for surgery to remove the infection below the skin's surface.

Jenny's sister and brother-in-law drove Jenny to Nashville. It was an emotionally-punishing two-hour drive. But through the uncertainty, she was feeling less driven by fear than by the determination to be at Jason's side. She wished that the drive would get her there faster. Jason's parents had gone before her, and she prayed that her husband would not be alone for very long.

The hospital staff was anxiously awaiting Jenny's arrival so that she could sign consent forms for Jason's surgery. The papers requested her permission for the surgeon to amputate if necessary and for Jason to receive a blood transfusion if needed. She signed them as soon as she arrived at the hospital, but she was still in denial, so the words did not resonate with her. She didn't believe that outcome was remotely possible. Young and naïve, she couldn't bring herself to believe that such horror could be cast upon good faithful people. God would not allow it.

Jenny was allowed to see Jason for a few short minutes while he was being prepped for surgery. When she saw him on the cold steel table in the hydro room, she sensed a vulnerability and helplessness unfamiliar to her. Before that, she had only seen a strong, determined man in her husband.

Jenny looked down at Jason and saw a single tear roll down his cheek and knew that he must be afraid. It was a heart-crushing moment, and she wanted more than anything to hold him close to her and cry uncontrollably. But that wasn't the show of strength that he needed from her. Instead, she chose to put on a brave front and reached down to tenderly kiss him and reassure him.

# THE PAIN OF LOSS

*"It's going to be hard, but hard is not impossible."*

**~ Chuck Palahniuk**

The hospital waiting room downstairs quickly filled with Jenny and Jason's families and several friends from their community. Jenny joined the large group to wait and pray. The love and faith were strong in the room, but they were all painfully unaware of what lay ahead. Jenny had emotionally blocked the worst of the possible outcomes, so she was unprepared for what was to come next.

In surgery, Dr. Guy faced a race to save Jason's life. The doctor knew Jason's right arm was too injured to be saved. But when he opened up Jason's left hand, it looked like a shotgun had gone off inside. The tendons from all ten figures of both hands were wrapped around Jason's wrists like rubber bands. They would never be functional again.

Dr. Guy entered the waiting room after working on Jason in surgery for hours. He asked for Jenny by name and approached her, looking so concerned that she knew the news he was about to deliver was not good. *"Jenny,"* he started. *"Jason's condition going into the surgery was a medical emergency. The infection was threatening to overwhelm and shut down his kidneys. I was forced to amputate his hands to save his life."*

The doctor's words didn't register at first. They couldn't be real. But when the reality of them came crashing down, she gasped for air as they engulfed her. Jenny fell to her knees and sobbed uncontrollably with her face buried in her hands. Her mind raced about wildly as she thought about how their lives had just changed. She questioned how in the world they were going to raise their girls. She wondered how they would pay for the house they had just bought from Jason's dad. More than anything, she feared for Jason's future and his quality of life. Losing one hand would have been an extraordinary challenge, but overcoming the loss of both hands seemed like a daunting task.

The first surgery was only the beginning of many to follow, though, and Jason's condition was still critical. Dr. Guy had been unsure if all of the infection was removed the first time and left the option open to remove more tissue if necessary. For the next three days, Jason was put into a medically-induced coma and underwent several surgeries. Each time, the doctor removed more and more of his arms in an attempt to reach the end of the toxic injured tissue that was causing the kidneys to react. At the end of the third day, the doctor was finally satisfied that he had accomplished the necessary removal of damaged tissue and infection. Jason's amputation was just below the elbows on both of his arms. Now, it was a matter of time.

After that third day, Jason was allowed to come out of his coma. He was groggy, and even though he was unaware of how much time had passed, he had enough recall to remember that he had been electrocuted. Lying in a hospital bed, he only wanted someone to level with him and tell him how badly he was injured. Shortly after he woke up, he asked to see his dad. He was close to him and knew that he would not mince words with him or try to sugarcoat the situation.

Through the obstruction of a feeding tube, Jason could only mumble his question. *"How bad is it?"* he asked. His dad looked down at him and answered, *"You know Jason, I don't know how, but we are going to get through this. It's going to be a hard road, but we have always had family and faith, and we will stick together and be fine."* Then as he continued, he laid out the extent of Jason's injuries with the directness Jason knew he could count on from him. *"They had to amputate both of your arms in order to save your life."* Jason looked up at his dad, and a tear ran down his cheek. Then, as peacefully as he'd awakened, he drifted back to sleep.

Several hours passed before Jason woke up for the second time. Though drowsy, he was completely aware of his condition. He knew he had lost both arms, and the thoughts of recovery went through his mind repeatedly. He kept thinking about his two little girls at home and knew he had to recover for them. He didn't know how yet, but there was no other option but to get to a point where he was contributing to their care and upbringing.

Dr. Guy entered the room, and for the first time, Jason met the man who was so dedicated to saving his life. *"Jason,"* he said pointedly. *"The road to recovery is going to be a difficult one for you. You are going to be here for possibly a month, maybe two."* Dr. Guy went on to explain how electricity works by burning from the inside out. For the first time, Jason was completely aware of just how fortunate he was. But he knew that his survival was divinely guided. He also knew there was a reason that he was spared. He would be dedicated to finding out what he was supposed to do with his life now.

Dr. Guy went on to tell Jason that, though his recovery was going to be hard, he needed to set realistic goals for himself—stepping-stones that were achievable. *"Jason, I work with my patients to help them reach one of their major goals while they are in my care. I want you to give some thought to what it is you want to achieve while you are here at the hospital, and you have my commitment to help you achieve that goal."* Jason's mind was racing, but he didn't need a lot of time to decide what his priority was.

As Dr. Guy headed to the door, about to leave the room, Jason abruptly stopped him. *"Dr. Guy! I know what I want."* The doctor stopped and returned to his seat next to the hospital bed. He was surprised that Jason had thought of something so quickly. It must be truly important for him to have reacted so fast. *"What do you want?"* he asked. *"How could you know what goal you want to reach when I just asked you?"* He had no way of knowing that Jason's daughters had been heavy on his mind since he woke up. *"Dr. Guy,"* he started. *"I have two little girls at home. I don't know if I will ever be able to dress or feed myself, but I have to be able to hold my girls again. It's all I care about."* Dr. Guy was both stunned and touched at the request. The two grown men cried together, both determined to reach Jason's goal. Neither knew the opportunity would present itself so soon.

A few days later, Jenny brought the two little girls to the hospital to see their daddy. Dr. Guy came into the room and announced their arrival. *"Would you like me to bring them in the room?"* he asked. *"Nope!"* Jason answered with no hesitation. *"Doctor, I cannot allow my girls to see me with all of these tubes hanging off of me. They are already going to be afraid. I want to go to the waiting room where I can appear as normal as possible to them."* Dr. Guy was shocked. He explained that he would have to disconnect Jason from all of the equipment he was attached to and questioned the decision to do so. Jason was defiant. *"I don't care!"* His strong will took over any other reasoning. He was going to do this. Dr. Guy could see the determination and heard it in Jason's voice. This was it. It was time to keep his promise. *"Okay,"* Dr. Guy said. *"Let's do this."*

After being disconnected from the equipment, Jason sat up in his bed for the first time. He felt a little woozy, but beyond that, he felt empowered. His smile was beaming from his wheelchair as he rounded the corner into the waiting room. When he saw his family there waiting for him, his heart was full. Each one of his girls was placed in his lap and held by the remnants of his arms. It was just as he had imagined. That was the moment that Jason thought to himself, *I've got this. Everything will be okay.* It had always been Jason's nature to believe that if you work hard enough, you can achieve anything. He experienced for one second in time a moment when his dad had entered his hospital room that he'd shed one small tear. That was it; there would be no more tears.

Immediately, Jason thought about getting out of the hospital to begin his new life. Dr. Guy told him that it would take a month or two to achieve the list of things that he needed to do in order to be released. Jason was determined as he had never been before to get through that list as quickly as possible. He simply responded to Dr. Guy with. *"Let's go!"* Jason was relentless in his work to make progress. He was also constant in his requests to be allowed to go home.

The entire time Jason spent in the hospital, Jenny was by his side, and his parents were there much of the time. They stayed in a local hotel to be close to him. Jason did not know who picked up the tab, but his family did not pay for the stay there.

Twelve days from the day Jason was hurt, Dr. Guy entered his room with the news. *"Jason,"* he said. *"I have never seen anyone work so hard to recover. I can't believe I am telling you this, but I am going to release you to go home."* The only stipulation was that Jenny would need to learn how to take care of him at home. In addition to the obvious healing of his arms, he had wounds on his legs where skin grafts were taken. There was a lot to be done, and Jenny was trained to bathe him and dress his wounds. She wanted him home, so she was committed to his care. Dr. Guy added one final thing. *"If I let you go home today, I want to be the one to take you to your car in the wheelchair."* Jason smiled and nodded.

Dr. Guy helped Jason into the wheelchair, and they exited the room into an L-shaped hallway. Waiting for them around the corner was every doctor, nurse, and resident in the hospital lined up against the walls to cheer him on. It was a proud moment.

Then for the first time in just under two weeks, Jason exited the hospital into the fresh spring air. He had a new appreciation for it.

Panther Creek Baptist Church was directly on the route home. The sign in front, normally reserved for scripture, said, "Welcome Home, Jason. We've been praying for you."

# DETERMINED TO LEARN

*"Courage does not always roar. Sometimes courage is the quiet voice at the end of the day saying I will try again tomorrow."*

**~ Mary Anne Radmacher**

Going home was a huge accomplishment in itself. Being there fostered a deep desire in Jason to continue to progress as he had through his hard work in the hospital. On his first day home, Jenny left to get groceries, and Jason's mom came to stay with him. The time passed painfully slowly as he contemplated everything he needed to relearn without the use of hands. He grew anxious with every passing minute and couldn't sit still, knowing there was so much to do to gain back his independence. Out of the corner of his eye, he spotted the keys to his truck and reached over to pick them up in his mouth. He mumbled to his mom that he wanted some time to himself, and he set out to see if he could get in his truck and start it up. He used every means available to unlock it and open the door. He struggled, but he was determined, using his teeth and his feet to see what would work. He needed to figure it out. Over and over, he fought with those keys. He'd dropped them repeatedly, and rather than give up, he would simply try again.

He had a rush of adrenaline when he finally got in but was then faced with the challenge to start the engine. He got the keys in the ignition using the same tactics that worked to help him unlock the door. Then, after a lot of additional trial and error, he got it started. Jason knew he shouldn't take the truck out on the street, so he settled on taking a single lap around the farm. It was a start. In fact, it was a big first step, and the accomplishment felt incredible. It had only been two weeks since the accident. It was the beginning of an era and his hope that he could get to a new normal quickly.

In the three months that followed, there was a meal delivered to the house every day. People that Jason and Jenny didn't even know brought food to the family. Sometimes, friends would just come to sit with Jason to give Jenny a break. The support of their friends, family, and community was overwhelming. It was welcome help during an unbelievably difficult time. God was putting people into their lives at the most strategic moments. A coworker showed up at their door and offered to pay some bills while another came by every week to clean the house.

Still, Jenny had to reach deep to find an inner strength beyond any that had ever been required of her before. She cared for the little girls and then for Jason, never once complaining. She would feed and bathe them all before ever having the opportunity to care for herself. The normal routine was already taxing, but she also had to clean and dress Jason's wounds twice every day. The cloth she used on one arm had to be discarded and replaced by a fresh one to clean the other, and more were needed for the wounds from the skin grafts on his legs to avoid cross-contamination. Keeping up with the laundry of the small family with the extra burden of wound care was a significant undertaking. Then, beyond all that was required at home, Jenny had to drive Jason to therapy twice a day.

Jenny prayed each day for God to just get her through the next one. She was both physically and emotionally exhausted every minute of every day. Going from being a young, vibrant couple to now one of them playing the role of a caretaker was extremely hard on the marriage. Jenny felt like they weren't even in a marriage. It was the most overwhelming and claustrophobic feeling Jenny had ever experienced. She felt smothered by all the care she had to give everyone else before having the time to care for herself. What's worse is that she could not visualize an ending. Would things ever get better? Never once did it occur to her to quit, but her heart ached for having to do things for Jason that neither of them should have had to experience in their relationship. Their love and commitment to each other were put to the test.

It is easy to see how the divorce rate for amputees is somewhere between eighty and ninety percent. The strain was overwhelming at times. But Jenny was deeply thankful that Jason was alive. Having him with her felt like an amazing miracle after almost losing him. She drew her strength from that feeling and from her deep faith. God had given them a second chance at life together as a family, and she needed him. Jason was her heart.

Jason received a prosthetic for his left arm relatively quickly. But the surgeries continued for his right arm for several more months, with him requiring additional skin grafts and corrective surgeries. The last one was finally completed the following December. Meanwhile, life was tough at home, and the undertaking to get to some semblance of a new normal was Jason's highest priority. The very first thing he needed to figure out was how to use the bathroom by himself. Having his mom or his wife help him was excruciatingly embarrassing and humiliating. In his mind, he felt like a burden worse than he'd ever felt in his life. He hated it!

The worst day of Jason's recovery, though, came during one of his first days' home when his small daughter wanted him to play a familiar game. When she cuddled next to him, he had always played counting her ribs and tickling her as he did. She crawled up in his lap and waited for the game to begin. That night, he couldn't play the game with her. After he put her to bed, he sat at the kitchen table and broke down for the first—and last—time. He knew that he needed to figure out how to do all of the things he'd previously known how to do—things that we all take for granted, and the truth is, he had taken them for granted too.

Jason was making progress on other tasks, tackling them one by one. In April, during turkey hunting season, his buddy, Sam, asked him to go with him to watch him hunt. Jason was eager to get out and let Jenny have the house to herself for the day, so he welcomed the opportunity. Once there, however, it was apparent that Sam had a different motive in mind. He laid a rifle in Jason's lap and told him he was going to hunt. Jason's immediate thought was that it was impossible. But Sam would not let it rest, and together, the two started to brainstorm about how to make it happen. Sam screwed a ratchet strap to the butt of the rifle and strapped it to Jason's shoulder. Then he put a V-shaped tripod on the front of the gun and attached it with a radiator hose clamp back to the shoulder strap so that when Jason turned, the gun would turn with him. Then he tied a string to the trigger and put it in Jason's mouth. When Jason pulled his chin down, the gun would fire. Now he could hunt. Jason shot his first turkey a month after his accident.

Every day brought with it a fresh opportunity for Jason to learn how to do more. There were trials and failures. Some days were not so good, and frustration would set in. But referring back to advice he had been given early on, he would never take his frustration out on his family. Instead, he would go for a walk to kick rocks and curse to himself before returning home. It was always his objective to walk back in that door with a renewed attitude and be happy for his family.

## PURPOSE AND BECOMING THE BEST

*"You have been assigned this mountain*
*so you can show others it can be moved."*

### ~ Mel Robbins

People often asked if Jason became stronger in his faith and closer to God during his recovery. His answer was always a simple *"no."* Nothing had changed for him; he was always strong in his faith. He had never questioned God's intention for him and never blamed God or asked why he had allowed this to happen to him. He simply felt that there was a reason for everything, and even though he didn't know what the purpose was, he needed to figure out what God intended for him to do with it. He would find out.

When Jason began to be fitted with his prosthetics by Arm Dynamics, he told the prosthetist that his goal was to be the best in the world at operating them. It was not sufficient to just "get by." Jason quickly found that he would need the best team of prosthetists and therapists working with him to reach that goal. Though every one of the early people he contacted did their best, some of them had not worked solely with upper prostheses and could not meet his goals. He continued to reach out to more and more of them until he found his dream team. Since that time, he has been told he now is the best in the world, but he chooses not to believe it. Instead. he continues to improve and learn new things every day.

About a year after the accident, Jason got his bionic arms. His prosthetist had ordered them, and his insurance company immediately rejected the request. But Jason would not take no for an answer. Typical to how Jason approached every challenge, he fought. He wrote many letters stating his case. He would be heard. Finally, he wrote a letter telling the insurance company that he was a father and wanted to continue to do his best, but that he could not even hold his little girl's hand to cross the street. That time, he reached someone and tugged at their heartstrings. They finally approved his bionics. He received them just under a year after his accident.

Touch Bionics was the bionics company at the time that manufactured the bionic hands for Jason. After receiving them, he was in the media a lot. The local news picked up his story and got the interest of CNN, who then also did a story. At the same time, *Hawaii Five-O* was interested in doing a remake of one of their most popular episodes from 1973 called *Hookman*. They wanted to update it by using bionic hands on the character instead of hooks. When they began to research and seek out someone who had double bionic hands, only one name surfaced. Jason was the only person in the world to have them. Following interviews and tests to review his capabilities, the show hired him.

Peter Weller, the director and the actor playing the villain in the episode, wanted Jason to do a couple of simple things like writing his name and holding a coffee cup. He and the producers were completely blown away by everything Jason was able to do. They asked him if he could build a sniper rifle. He didn't know but said he would try. As is typical for Jason, he gave it everything he had. Of course, he was successful at doing that, so they came up with several additional things for him to do that they would have otherwise had to tackle through production in a mocked-up setting. He tackled a laundry list of requests, from aiming that rifle to picking up a coffee cup. In one scene, he sat behind Peter, reaching his bionic arm through Peter's to look like it belonged to the actors, then reached up to remove his glasses. Everything he accomplished was filmed for the show. Peter got much more than he had hoped for. Jason was originally scheduled to film for three days and ended up on set filming for two and a half weeks.

Peter and Jason became good friends and exchanged phone numbers. Then Jason wondered, *how do you call a famous actor? Do you call them every day or never call them?* After Jason returned home, Peter called *him*. He said, *"Hey Jason, did you know that Touch Bionics has come out with a new hand?"*

*"Yeah, I know,"* Jason answered. *"But my insurance is never going to approve them. They are $150,000 each. It's just not going to happen."* Peter asked Jason if he knew anyone at *Touch Bionics*, and at the time, he didn't. The conversation left his mind, and he didn't give it another thought.

A few days later, Peter called Jason again and told him he would be receiving a call from *Touch Bionics*. Jason was not expecting what Peter told him next. He simply asked him, *"Why?"* Peter said, *"I told them that if they wanted their name mentioned on Hawaii Five-O that they better get you hooked up with a new set of hands."* Jason was shocked. *"Are you kidding me?"* *"No!"* Peter said. *"If they want the publicity, they are going to earn it."* Touch Bionics then set him up with a new set of hands.

When Touch Bionics saw the show, they immediately contacted Jason. Skeptical, they wanted to know if Jason had really been able to do the tasks or if it was a simple setup for TV. They had never seen anyone who could use prosthetics like Jason could and asked him if he would do some testing with them. They flew Jason to a facility in Ohio and began testing his abilities. They began with a series of tests that involved simple tasks like unlocking a door. In many cases, it took him less time than someone who had both of their natural hands. They were so amazed by his abilities that they consulted him when developing new products. They would have him use the product for a couple of months and have him review it, asking what he liked and disliked, in addition to what his wish list would be. He was eventually giving his input directly to the product engineers.

Jason began representing Touch Bionics in other capacities. One of his early assignments was introducing a fourth-generation hand to the world at a news conference in Leon, France. Then, upon returning to the US, he helped to introduce the product here. Touch Bionics was bought out by Ossur, a company located in California. Jason is a product ambassador for them now. He attends most of the amputee shows with them to show their products. Jason has been around the world as a speaker to inspire other amputees.

His inspirational message is one of overcoming and learning to be the best you can be while working with the cards you are dealt. He talks about the importance of not quitting. He says, *"You have to be willing to learn and keep at it."*

Jason has also used his experience to help teach an important life lesson to his kids. When they ask questions about what happened to him, he tells them that life is not perfect. *"When something happens that you don't like, learn from it and go on. There are always going to people that have a better car or a better house. Sometimes, you may feel like they don't deserve it. Then you might begin to wonder why something like my accident happens to a good person. But life is not fair, and it is never going to be."*

Jason's tenacity, determination, and confident mindset are all truly inspirational traits. He will tell you, though, that his faith is his greatest strength.

———————

## YOUR GAME PLAN:

Are you facing a disabling injury?

- Reach out to resources experienced with disabling injuries and to local organizations dedicated to helping individuals live with a new disability. The website www.ablethrive.com is an example of a hub for support resources. Many more are available online.

- Manage mental challenges – www.helpguide.org is one of many nonprofit organizations that help people find resources to help with mental health challenges. See the "Winning Points" section for more from this valuable website.

- The following article in Help Guide is worth the read. *Living Well with a Disability, Author: Melinda Smith, M.A.* June 2019, https://www.helpguide.org/articles/healthy-living/living-well-with-a-disability.htm.

- What new skills do you need to learn? Where will you get that instruction? Ask for help on this step if you need it.

www.amputee-coalition.org is an organization that Jason works with. Their mission:

"To reach out to and empower people affected by limb loss to achieve their full potential through education, support and advocacy, and to promote limb loss prevention."

(Read the "Winning Points" below, then re-visit this exercise for any additions that may be prompted by the review of that section.)

## WINNING POINTS:

When I asked Jason what one piece of advice he would give to an amputee or any other individual fighting to overcome such a big challenge, he said, *"Always have faith. God knew I could get through my situation. I believe that people who suffer tragedy and don't do well don't lean on God enough. Not everyone is blessed with family like I am. They need to know they have somewhere to turn."*

JENNY TALKS ABOUT COPING IN THE FIRST YEAR:

*"The journey is long, but it is 100% possible to get better."*

**~ Jenny Koger**

- Praying for the strength to get through "Tomorrow" one day at a time – *"Bad things happen to good people."* Jenny believes that by putting this on her life, God spoke through her. When people asked how she got through it. She says that she could not have done it without her faith. *"There was no other answer."*

## HEALING AND MOVING FORWARD

- **Accept help from others** – It's human nature to want independence. But when we are struggling, having others to help us meet our goals and think through our concerns and plans can help us progress faster than we are capable of on our own.

- **Celebrate Success** – Even small successes are worthy of celebration when faced with a major setback. Celebrate with others too. An enthusiastic pat on the back can help your self-esteem and keep you pushing forward.

- **Fail forward** – Recognize failures as a stepping stone toward success and as a guide for what not to do the next time around. Frustration is normal, and it's okay to feel it once in a while. But it's important to move away from that mindset as quickly as possible. Use that feeling to spur your determination. Practice your self-talk carefully here. Repeat after me: "I can do this!" Say it often.

## JASON ON FAILURE:

*"You have to be willing to learn. People look at me as the best prosthetic user in the world. But I failed many times before I experienced success. Life is not perfect; everybody fails at something sometimes. You need to learn something from every failure. If you let it beat you up, you are never going to get past your challenges."*

- **Set realistic goals** – It's okay to set big goals. In fact, it should be encouraged. But make sure your goals are attainable. Consistently take small steps to reach that larger goal.

- **Believe in yourself** – Once you have set attainable goals, believe that you can achieve them. Here's where that self-talk comes into play again. Write down your affirmations and practice them several times a day. For help with understanding and creating affirmations read *The Power of Affirmations & the Secret to Their Success* by Louise Shapely. You can find this book and other resources on Amazon.

## HANDING BACK

Jason and Peter continue to be friends and talk at least once a month. Peter told Jason that he wanted to come to Owensboro, Jason's hometown, and meet the community and people who have helped Jason get to where he is today. So, Peter flew into town, and Jason coordinated an event coinciding with his arrival called *"Handing Back."* They charged ten dollars each for admittance. They raised $18,000 at that first event, which Jason gave to seven different local charities. When Peter returned for a second event, they raised $21,000, which Jason gave to elementary schools to fill their Christmas wish lists.

Jason is also involved with Amputee Coalition. Amputees from all over the world reach out to him. He personally answers every email and returns every call because he has a strong desire to help and make a difference. Jason also does public speaking, both for Ossur and on his own. He gets many requests. A lot of the funds he receives he uses to help others. His family has a history of faith and charitable giving. Jason has been told he gives a little too much sometimes. But giving is embedded in his core, and he won't have it any other way.

Today, Jason tells his inspirational story by speaking to amputee groups. Also, when Vanderbilt University Medical Center in Nashville (where he had his surgery) admits a new amputee, they contact Jason. He makes a two-hour drive to the hospital to visit with the patient as a volunteer. He gives the patients hope by showing them what he can do with his artificial arms and explaining how he overcame to live a full life. Jason says he loves doing this the most above anything else.

## EXTRA POINT:

Arm Dynamics: www.armdynamics.com

Ossur: www.ossur.com

**Alice Sullivan** - Special thanks to Alice Sullivan for introducing me to Jason and his amazing story. Alice is an extremely talented ghostwriter. You can learn more about her on her website. www.alicesullivan.com

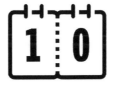

## FINAL SCORE:

Jason wants the public to know that he is accessible and will answer all emails and inquiries.

He lives with his wife, Jenny, and their three children in Owensboro, Kentucky. He maintains a website at www.jasonkoger.com. You can locate his email there and view some of his videos and pictures. He says he is always is happy to talk with others about amputation and prosthetic limbs.

On Instagram he is at @kroger84, and on Facebook he's @jasonkogerofficial

Subscribe to Jason's YouTube channel, where he shares a portion of his life with his viewers and offers advice and instruction to other amputees.

www.youtube.com/channel/UCwznconKfLCUhipttJ3QeDg

## FORWARD PASS:

*The first story in the fourth quarter is about growth through adversity. It has an important lesson about trust and making sure you know the integrity of those you work for. Matthew Overlund utilized his important life lessons to train others, and then to write an amazing book about leadership.*

*The last story is not as much about beating your own challenges, but more about helping others overcome theirs. It's about growing enough in your career that you are capable of paying your experience and knowledge forward. Giving back and investing in others is the final lesson.*

---

# FOURTH QUARTER

## GROWTH AND GIVING BACK

*"At the end of the day, it's not about what you have
or even what you've accomplished . . .
It's about who you've lifted up—who you've made better.
It's about what you've given back."*

**~ Denzel Washington**

## FOURTH QUARTER CHAMPION QUALITIES:

* Growth          * Failing Forward       * Investing in others

* Trust           * Self-Confidence       * Work Ethic

* Self-Value      * Gratitude             * Relationship Building

* Communication Skills

# MATTHEW
# OVERLUND

---

# CHAPTER SEVEN

# A CORPORATE CHAMPION

*"Givers have to set limits because takers rarely do."*

~ **Irma Kurtz**

# MATTHEW OVERLUND'S STORY

## VICE PRESIDENT OF PRODUCT DEVELOPMENT, CONCORD TECHNOLOGIES

*(Some names have been changed)*

Fired! Matt was stunned. He had worked for the small tech company for fifteen years, and in that time, he'd invested an obscene amount of his personal time toward its success. Bryce, the business owner, recognized that the company's future growth was dependent on Matt's continued contribution. That is what he told Matt when he offered him an equity share of the business. In reality, that was a bribe meant to keep Matt working at a level of commitment far beyond that of a regular employee. The partnership offer was just an empty promise.

Now at the airport, Matt was about to fly home from Miami to Bend, Oregon, when the reality of what had happened in a hotel meeting room a few hours earlier started to sink in. He was in Florida working at the company user conference. The morning after wrapping up that event, he and Bryce walked together into a meeting set up earlier under the pretense of discussing a possible merger.

When they arrived at the meeting, Matt noticed a sheriff standing in the hallway and had a passing thought that it was a little weird. Then, when he entered the room, he saw the company's attorney, Jeff, seated at an oddly oversized table that took up almost the entire conference room. Matt knew Jeff, and it didn't seem unusual for him to be there, considering they were about to discuss a possible acquisition. But there was another man in the room that Matt didn't know. Jeff introduced him as another attorney from his office. Bryce took a seat next to the two attorneys on one side of the table and asked Matt to be seated across from them. The entire setting was beginning to feel strange.

Jeff started to speak and didn't mince words as he got straight to the point. *"Matt, we have several things to talk to you about this morning, but you need to know beforehand that this conversation will end with your termination from the company."* Matt was in shock and could only sit motionless as he listened. He hung on every word but was so stunned and unprepared for what was taking place that if asked at that moment, he wouldn't have been able to respond without tripping over his words.

Matt and Bryce had been at odds over several issues for a while. He suspected that Bryce was considering his termination, but given his history, he thought it would be a mutual, more amicable separation that would take place further down the road. He was in complete disbelief that this was happening now and in this hostile setting.

It seemed a bit extreme for Bryce to sit by and watch the company attorney act as the axman. But things started to make a little more sense as Jeff continued. He launched into a laundry list of Matt's supposed wrongdoings that ranged from the misuse of company resources to violating the company's non-disclosure agreement. Matt felt his blood pressure rise, becoming more and more enraged at the accusations. He had made so many personal sacrifices for Bryce's company in the preceding years, and being dismissed like this was unconscionable.

Matt had started consulting for Bryce and his partner, Joel, at their small document imaging company as a side job while he was in the Marines. The year was 1998, and he was doing development work for the then two-man operation. Even then, he displayed his strong work ethic by the number of hours he worked. He was committed from the start to help the small company succeed, and the excessive hours set the tone for the balance of his tenure. When he was honorably discharged from the Marines in 1999 because of a previously undetected heart problem, Bryce offered him a full-time position.

Over time, the three men were successful at growing the business and developing products to meet the market demand of the industry. They were becoming so successful that they were getting noticed by industry leaders. It was one of those companies that proposed buying the business and made an offer they couldn't refuse. About four years after Matt first started working with the company, the partners agreed to sell.

The sale was contingent upon the buying company being acquired by another of the industry giants at the same time. But 9/11 happened, and the sale fell through because of the economic uncertainty surrounding the terrorist attack. As a result, the whole deal was scrapped. Matt's company had hired a handful of employees during their growth but let all of them go when their half of the sale was imminent. But then, they were stuck and forced to start from scratch. They needed to begin hiring everyone back. Fast!

Matt's brother, Brandon, was among the first to come back. Before the failed sale, Matt had taken on additional responsibilities for the Support and QA departments. He needed to stay focused on the company's lifeline in product development, so to free up some of his time, he hired Brandon to take on the support team.

Things started to get back to business as usual as more of the employees returned. But Joel, who had seen the sale as an opportunity to move on to other things, decided to go ahead and leave the company. Bryce bought him out and then presented Matt with a verbal proposal to partner with him. But he didn't put an offer or the terms of an agreement in writing. Matt trusted Bryce and knew they would get around to it.

With Joel's departure, the company needed an accounting professional, and Matt's wife, Miranda, had the perfect background to fill the position, reporting directly to Bryce. Other jobs were more challenging to fill. Over the year's salespeople had come and gone. But when the company finally found Sean, they had found someone who possessed both skill and longevity. Not only was Sean a great hire, but over time, he and Matt became trusted friends.

As technology was changing, more and more employees could work remotely from home. Bryce moved the operation to Florida, along with his residence. The California office was closed. Matt and Miranda moved to Portland to be closer to family and began working from there. Sean continued to work remotely from his home in Northern California.

The workload was not reduced with the change for Matt, though. Matt and his team worked crazy hours to pull off seemingly impossible feats. The company was landing impressive contracts through their efforts. Even so, Bryce showed little appreciation for his team's sacrifices, focusing only on small mistakes that would be inevitable with any level of achievement. As a result, the relationship between Bryce and Matt continued to suffer.

## BROKEN PROMISES

*"A verbal contract isn't worth the paper it's written on."*

### ~ Samuel Goldwyn

After Sean had been with the company for a few years, he had conversations with Bryce about an equity arrangement. Bryce again avoided putting anything in writing, though. Still, trusting that their contributions were somehow adding credit to their equity share, Matt and Sean didn't push the topic often. They should have. They were almost single-handedly beefing up the company's bottom line. When the subject of a written agreement did come up, Bryce said it was a complicated issue that he would work out with the legal team.

Meanwhile, neither were being included in any of the company's major decisions. Matt's knowledge of the finances was limited to what Miranda told him from her work in the accounting department. She was reporting some questionable indulgences, and even though the transactions were not illegal, it was spending that would typically be discussed within any true partnership. The lack of transparency of the company's financials was starting to raise Matt's suspicions. He was beginning to think Bryce might be trying to secure their continued commitment under an equity partnership pretext.

Matt and Sean began to push Bryce harder to make good on his promises to them. After that continued pressure, Bryce finally drafted an equity and partnership contract. But the financial requirements for the agreement were not realistic for Matt or Sean, and Bryce knew it. They didn't have that kind of money. What's worse is that beyond that buy-in requirement, Bryce was only offering them a combined fifteen percent of the company's equity. It was laughable.

Matt leaned back in his chair after reviewing the contract and gripped the armrests so hard that his knuckles were white. Then, as Sean shot him a look of mutual disapproval, he reached over and shoved the paperwork back across the table. *"This is bullshit!"* he said sternly. *"We have poured our life's blood into this company for years with the understanding that as partners, we were banking a portion of the earnings. You haven't given us credit for any of the profits we have helped you earn. It's like we are starting from scratch."*

It was hard for Matt to imagine that Bryce would think that this agreement could even come close to satisfying him. Bryce had promised Sean and him that their hard work was an investment that would pay them back in dividends. But according to the agreement, that was not the case. They were furious!

Bryce was taking them for granted, but he also desperately needed them, so he'd been leading them on. Of course, he understood loud and clear that they were not happy with the agreement and tried to appease them by promising that he would go back and try again. But what he was trying to do was buy more time. Bryce did not make a second attempt at a contract until almost a year later.

The second contract wasn't much better than the first, and honestly, even if it had been an amazing offer, the two would not have accepted it. At that point, so much water was under the bridge that Matt and Sean had finally had enough. They decided that it was time to form their own company to personally profit from their talents. It was clear that was not going to happen while they continued to work for Bryce. They planned to give Bryce plenty of notice and would leave him as prepared as they possibly could.

They started to execute their plan by designing a website and logo with the help of a friend, Jason, who was an artist who had consulted for Bryce's company for years. During that time, Matt and Jason built a trusted friendship. But Jason was also friends with Bryce, and to complicate things further, his wife, Jennifer, also worked for Bryce's company in QA in a position reporting to, you guessed it, Matt. Thus, Jason and Jennifer were dependent on the company for a large portion of their income, and the relationships were complicated. Matt and Sean should have realized that they had shaped the perfect storm for deception and personal gain. Matt's motive was not malicious, but he was utilizing resources that were creating conflicting loyalties. He would soon fully realize the impact of that mistake.

Several months into the new venture, Matt arrived in Florida to work at the company's second annual user conference. There had been some strange occurrences before the event. In hindsight, they should have been tell-tale signs of what was to come. First, during the previous week, he wasn't getting responses from Jason or Jennifer when he called them. It was like they had fallen off the face of the earth. What's worse, some of Jennifer's work was not getting done. When he was finally able to reach them, the response he got was startling. They informed him that they had been off-line because they were in the middle of relocating to Florida. Matt didn't even know they were moving. There was no attempt to explain what had prompted the move and no apologies for the uncompleted work. According to them, Bryce had cleared everything. The inference was that they didn't need to inform him or even keep him in the loop. It felt very suspicious.

Meanwhile, Bryce instructed Matt and Sean to change their flights to leave the day after the conference. He told them that he needed to discuss a possible merger and acquisition with them and wanted to meet face to face with them while they were in town. That seemed fairly routine, but Matt would not understand the irony of how Bryce positioned the meeting until later.

Matt and Sean were having multiple conversations at that point and knew that something strange was going on. To further their suspicions, they were booked to stay in a different hotel tower than the rest of the employees. They were isolated.

All of the evidence pointed to their termination. Still, they believed the exit would be in a matter of months, not days, and it would be through a mutual agreement. For now, they agreed that they had a job to do and would deal with whatever was going on after the conference. Matt went about his normal routine. Dealing with the employees and customers was business as usual, but the tension among the executive team was exceedingly apparent.

Then, the morning after the conference close, Matt was at the scheduled meeting sitting across the table from Bryce and his attorney henchmen. It was an ambush! Jeff, one of Bryce's attorneys, continued speaking. *"We are aware that you and Sean have been working on a side project to start your own company."*

*"You are planning to develop a product that will directly compete with this company's products, and you used company resources to execute that plan,"* Jeff said pointedly. *"We have already prepared a lawsuit and are ready to file it unless you agree to abandon that plan. Unless you agree to our terms,"* he continued, *"you will also renounce the severance package we are offering you."*

There was no defending the use of company resources, even though those contacts had become personal friends over the years. Matt realized that he should have used better judgment, but his intentions were not accurate as they were being presented. It was not his plan for the product he was developing to compete with any that Bryce's company sold. Further, he had planned for his exit to be mutual and then peacefully leave.

Bryce fixed his eyes on Matt. He looked confidently smug and seemed to be relishing in the foolish "gotcha" moment. Matt had given so much to the company. He was livid! Still, he said little in his defense, knowing that to do so would only escalate the situation. There was no one friendly to him in the room. Thus, he was not about to offer up any information.

It was evident that seating him at an oversized conference room table with two attorneys present and a sheriff standing guard outside the door was all meant to be intimidating. He knew that they were not concerned about his reaction or what he might do. They simply wanted him to be afraid of them.

During the process, Matt realized that Jason had turned over all of his company startup plans to Bryce. Some of the information Jeff was citing could not have come from any other source. In return for his loyalty, Bryce moved Jennifer and him to Florida and set them up to live there. From the point of gaining the information from Jason, Bryce's out-of-control imagination took off like a misguided missile.

Many of Bryce's suspicions were so farfetched that they were laughable. In fact, Matt did laugh out loud a couple of times at some of the ridiculous accusations and at the fact that Bryce and Jeff were so sure of themselves. He wasn't convinced that Bryce bought into some of the absurd rhetoric either. Given Bryce's character, it was more realistic that he felt betrayed and had a bruised ego. But he was most angry that Matt and Sean were taking their talent to start their own company, and he would no longer be at the helm. They had been among his best talent, and they might be successful without him.

Matt asked for a few hours to read through the paperwork, including a copy of the lawsuit and a severance agreement. The agreement stated that the lawsuit would be terminated if he waived

204 | SURROUNDED BY CHAMPIONS

all of his rights to the new company and turned over everything associated with it.

After Sean had his turn in the hot seat, he and Matt put their heads together and contacted an attorney to review the documents, including the demand to abandon their plans or risk being sued. The attorney told them that it was unlikely that Bryce could enforce all of his demands but that it would cost a lot of time and money to fight. They didn't have the funds to fight, and Bryce knew it.

Matt signed the agreement to avoid entering into a battle that he didn't have the means to win. He let go of his dreams of independence and freedom with the stroke of a pen. Instead, he settled for a small severance check and uncertainty about his future. The crushing defeat he felt was devastating.

# MINDSET & CHANGE

*"Knowing your value is important,*
*but it's more important not to allow it*
*to be defined by someone else."*

**~ Matthew Overlund**

Matt left the hostile environment at the hotel behind him and stepped outside into the bright Florida sunshine to head home. The morning events left him dazed, but he hadn't been exposed to fresh air since he arrived, and he allowed his mind to escape while he relished in it. There was a steady breeze, and the surrounding palm trees rustled above him. He paused for a moment to admire the tall, hovering giants and grappled with the thought that he would most likely not return there again any time soon.

The drive to the airport was a blur. Once he stepped into the TSA security line, he became panic-stricken at the realization that his entire household income and everything he had worked so hard for had all been wiped out in a single day. His years of committed work would be diminished to a sales pitch on his resumé.

When handing the TSA agent his documents, his hands were so shaky that he felt he should explain that he had just been fired. The agent raised an eyebrow, looked over him briefly, and gave him a sympathetic, "Sorry about that, pal," expression and continued to push him through the checkpoint. Embarrassed for having said anything, Matt awkwardly chuckled to himself. Apparently, he didn't look threatening enough to have any explosives or drugs. He would have a good laugh about the exchange later. Much later.

During the flight home, Matt's mind raced as he recalled the details of the morning meeting. Bryce had shaken his confidence badly. Of course, his abilities had not changed in the course of just a few hours, but that didn't stop him from questioning them. He wondered if he had not been as skilled as he thought he was. Then he was angry at himself for having such ridiculous thoughts and allowing Bryce to undermine his value and shake his self-confidence. He needed to shift his mindset to find the right job. The question was whether or not he could.

Looking for a job was uncharted territory for Matt. After his service in the Marines, he had only ever worked for Bryce. He had considered taking all of his and Miranda's savings and combining it with his severance to still go out on his own. But he didn't have any experience in sales and marketing. The partnership with Sean had offered a way around that. But with that off the table, how could he become an entrepreneur without the ability to sell his product?

In the end, Matt determined that going out on his own was too risky, and he accepted a job offer that had been on the table before he left Florida. His brother, Brandon, called an industry contact to let them know that Matt was unexpectedly available, and a job offer came almost immediately. It was a verbal offer made on a moment's notice, and the details were not hammered out yet, but there was no questioning the company wanted him. That in itself should have bolstered his confidence.

He received the details of the offer a few days later. It turned out that there was a price to pay for accepting that job, as the salary was considerably less than what he had earned in his previous position. But with his self-confidence still shaken and no other offers immediately on the table, he felt that accepting it was his best option.

A few months after accepting the job, his friend, Sean, came back into the picture in a big way. He called Matt to tell him about a job opportunity where he worked in Seattle and wanted to recommend Matt for that job. *"Would you be interested?"* he asked. Matt was *very* interested. He was overqualified and underpaid for the position he had accepted. Even though he knew it at the time, he hadn't expected the heavy feelings of boredom and being underutilized. He had only been at that job for six months when he decided to accept a position working at Sean's company.

Matt felt like he was at the starting gate all over again. But he had originally interviewed for a position he knew he was overqualified for. The company recognized this too and offered him a position with more responsibility and authority. Even though accepting the higher position would have meant closing the financial gap, he could not take it in good faith. He didn't feel he could do the position justice until he became acclimated to the new company. He took the lower role, understanding that he would move up in the ranks when it made more sense to him personally.

It took Matt a year to climb his way back up to receive that promotion. Still, Matt recognized that the job was not going to last forever or be his last stop. The job didn't fully match his long-term goals, and because of that, he only worked there for two years before deciding it was time to move on again.

After years of work in the industry, Matt was very well known. He had developed hundreds of business contacts that remained constant even as he moved from job to job. Despite his history with Bryce, his reputation was one for having a unique talent in product development and possessing an excellent work ethic.

When Concord Technologies was searching for a Director of Product Strategy, they reached out to their industry network for recommendations. (Concord Technologies is Matt's employer as of this writing.)

Mitch was a business friend of Matt's, and had worked with him as a customer over the years. They had not had face-to-face contact in a while but remained friends through social media. Mitch was one of the associates that Concord reached out to in their search for the product strategy candidate. He told them that he would think about his contacts over the upcoming weekend and get back to them.

When Mitch contacted Concord the following week, he told them that he only knew of one person who had the talent and capabilities to fill the position. He, of course, was referring to Matt.

Matt went through an interview with the chief commercial officer that stretched well beyond what would normally take one to five hours over multiple sessions. He thoroughly impressed the executive with his product and industry knowledge. There was no question that he had a lot of talent to bring to the company, and his work ethic was legendary, as evidenced by Mitch's recommendation. He received an offer and accepted the position.

Matt was recently promoted and has responsibility for the engineering team located in India in addition to product management. That promotion put him in charge of both the functional and technical sides of one of the company's major products.

Long before his current role came about, Matt was working on his dream to be an author. Focusing on that goal, he joined a mastermind of other authors and aspiring authors and continued to seek out other people's expertise through books and online courses.

In early 2020, Matt launched his first book, *Stop Pulling the Ship*. Matt drew from his years of experience as a manager and the lessons he learned along the way. It is a guide on leadership directed specifically at new managers and building teams.

Matt follows his own advice and strives to make his team members more autonomous. He says that selfishly (his word, not mine), he doesn't want to work with a team full of people who need to constantly be told how to do their jobs. It is too time-consuming, and it means that he cannot do other things that interest him because he is reduced to merely managing tasks.

> *"You must always look for ways to increase autonomy*
> *and engagement in your team.*
> *If you can do that, you will have a successful team*
> *that can take care of itself."*
>
> **~ Matthew Overlund**

Matt continues to support his teams at Concord and is grateful to have found a company that appreciates his efforts. Someday though, most likely after retirement, he will leave his teams to benefit from the years of training he has given them to fulfill his dream to write full-time. We just may be lucky enough to be able to read his first fiction before then.

## YOUR GAME PLAN:

What does your future hold?

- If you are in a leadership role, training employees to perform in those roles, or are working with teams, read Matt's book,

*Stop Pulling the Ship*. It contains valuable advice for both new and seasoned leaders.

- What are some clues that you are about to be fired? The steps to take if you get fired. (See "Winning Points," below.)

- If you have been promised an equity position or profit-sharing, get that agreement in writing. Be sure to check your state's labor laws.

- Are all of your income streams positioned in one basket? Read Rachel Richards's books, *Money Honey* and *Passive Income Aggressive Retirement*, to learn about creating passive income and developing other income streams. Rachel offers valuable advice on money management.

- What new skills do you need to learn to meet your goals? Where will you get that instruction? Books, mentors, podcasts, coaches, masterminds, classes? You guessed it, research these, and put together your game plan.

(Read the "Winning Points" below, then re-visit this exercise for any additions that may be prompted by the review of that section.)

## WINNING POINTS:

As of this writing, Matt and I are in a mastermind together, and I consider him to be inspirational and a personal friend. I have read his book from cover to cover. It is exceptional and one of the best books that I have read on leadership and team building (I read a lot!). I was so impressed with his message that I read it in a matter of days.

The six areas Matt explores in the section of his book entitled *Transforming Your Team* are as follows in a modified version: (I encourage you to buy the book for the full content if you are interested in this important topic.)

*"To be an effective leader, you must take definitive and intentional actions to guide your team and empower them with the necessary support and structure they need."*

~ **Matthew Overlund,** *Stop Pulling the Ship*

- **Motivation:** Matt says you need to understand why each individual on the team connects with their work to discover how to best leverage and take advantage of their innate motivation to succeed.

- **Success:** The book explains that success is more than getting things done. It's about getting the right things done at the right time. Matt stresses that to do that, you need to establish a framework (a written plan) that clearly spells out the process that will lead to an expected result.

- **Failure:** *"Even the best teams will fail."* Matt says, *"Neglect to plan for a failure, and the most promising team may fall apart when facing its first significant challenge."* He suggests that it isn't wise to forge ahead blindly but instead have a plan to overcome obstacles.

- **Personnel Changes:** Sometimes you do not have the right person to fill a given role on your team. Matt emphasizes that you must be willing and able to leverage personnel changes as a positive and powerful tool for building a successful team. He will also tell you, *"It's not easy!"*

- **Delegating Responsibility:**

> *"The difficulty of a task*
> *has no bearing on your responsibility to complete it."*

> ~ **Matthew Overlund,** *Stop Pulling the Ship.*

The point here, according to Matt, is that you have a responsibility to delegate work to your team while giving them the means to successfully complete the work objective. By the way, understand that you can't do everything yourself. Delegate!

- **Three Elements of Successful Delegation:**

1. Autonomy: You must give your team the freedom to "evaluate, plan, and execute" the work they are responsible for.

2. Authority: This is closely aligned with autonomy. Trust your team to complete their work without continually inserting yourself in the decision-making.

3. Accountability: In the book, Matt highlights the concept that your team should take on the tasks that they want to work on, but that they should understand that each individual is accountable to the group as a whole for their contribution.

## FOUR KEY INDICATORS THAT YOU ARE ABOUT TO BE FIRED

1. **Declining relationship with your boss:** This doesn't always happen over the course of years as it did for Matt and his boss, Bryce. Sometimes, you don't hit it off with a boss right out of the starting gate. Regardless of the timing, if you

212 | SURROUNDED BY CHAMPIONS

are not getting along with the person you report to, it is inevitable that a change is coming. Chances are, your boss will not be the one to leave.

2. **Isolation:** If your peers or subordinates avoid you like the plague, they may know something about your future with the company you don't. In Matt's case, he and Sean were separated from the rest of the employees at the hotel where they were staying for their company event. Then, while at the conference, the other managers were distant. Both of these were major indicators that his longevity was in jeopardy.

3. **Exclusion from meetings or key decisions:** If you are suddenly not being invited to meetings or included in decisions that would normally fall within your area of responsibility, it is a warning sign that you may be on your way out.

4. **Your job performance is being documented:** (not in a good way)

   If your employer wants to terminate you, they will want to create a document trail as supporting evidence for their decision. If you are suddenly receiving written warnings on your job performance, beware.

# FOUR STEPS TO TAKE
# IF YOU ARE FIRED

1. **Update your resumé:** There are a ton of online resources and professionals to help.

2. **Connect with your inner circle:** Be sure to check with your friends and family. Many times, they will have a good job lead for you.

3. **Conduct your job search:** Again, there are online resources like www.monster.com, www.indeed.com, and others.

4. **Prepare to interview:** Be sure to do your research on the company you are interviewing with. Then search online for practice questions. Bottom line, be prepared!

(Don't wait to take action if you already see any of the warning signs above. It is easier to find a job while you still have one because you don't have to explain the firing in an interview, and there is less pressure to immediately replace your income.)

## LEARNING NEW SKILLS

Matt promised himself that he would never be in a position again where he couldn't make what he knew to be the right decision because he was ill-equipped to execute it. He would teach himself the skills he needed. Then, he spent several years closing that gap as he immersed himself in books and listened to speakers.

## EXTRA POINT:

Rachel Richards: Before putting her own system to work, Rachel was working for a verbally abusive boss in a job she hated. She now teaches others how to earn passive income and find financial freedom. By the way, she retired at the age of 27, and she will tell you how. Connect with Rachel at www.moneyhoneyrachel.com

## FINAL SCORE:

You can email Matt at: matt@leadershipandvision.com

Buy Matt's book, *Stop Pulling the Ship*, at Amazon.com

To learn more about Matt and how he teaches management and leadership skills, or to check out his blog, visit www.leadershipandvision.com.

## FORWARD PASS:

*The last story is my own. I write about how I prepared my office for my retirement and how much pleasure I experienced while training my replacement. This final message is about how fulfilling it is to share experience and knowledge to help a champion find success.*

# CHRISTA GETZ
# AND
# KAREN HUNSANGER

(Retirement party June 14, 2019 Sacramento, CA)

---

# CHAPTER EIGHT

# TWO MINUTE WARNING ~ READY TO RETIRE

### INVEST IN OTHERS TO MAKE MORE MONEY, FIND SUCCESS, AND EXPERIENCE MORE FREEDOM AND JOY.

# THE INTERVIEW

*"First impressions never have a second chance"*

### ~ Charles R Swindoll

I was stunned when I entered the room. As my eyes swept the small office, I took in every detail of the space. What office hell had I just entered?

This was clutter disguised as a workspace, and I attempted to make sense of the unconventional layout. Oddly out of place and almost blocking the entrance was an oversized, glass-topped octagon-shaped dining room table. It stood butted up against a large U-shaped reception-style desk that was surprisingly functional in the midst of the chaos. Together, the two pieces of furniture took up almost half of the already-limited office space.

On the adjacent wall was an overstuffed bookcase that was the disorganized storage area for office supplies. Each of the four shelves was precariously stacked to the extent that the contents were unidentifiable from a distance. To say it looked like a hoarder's dream is an understatement. Worse, it was the focal point when first walking through the door.

Situated next to the bookcase were four tall, mismatched, and badly beaten file cabinets. Judging by their leaning, decrepit condition, I was sure that at least two of them had been relocated from the warehouse after first being rammed by a forklift. The contents were spilling from the tops of the jarred drawers, some of which could not be completely closed.

Two doors exited the room. One led to the warehouse and was positioned on the far wall next to a credenza. On the worn surface of the credenza was the community coffee maker and some random kitchen supplies. The other door led into an adjoining office and had a water cooler next to it. This workplace desperately needed a designated, organized kitchen area. Further, to be taken seriously as a business, it should have been furnished with professional-looking furniture instead of with someone's garage sale outcasts. It looked like an office afterthought rather than a professional space.

I was entirely unprepared for what came next. My eyes met with the true office treasures. (Please note the sarcasm.) The crown jewels were two pictures that measured about three feet by three feet each and together took up almost an entire wall. They appeared to be abstract renditions of streets and buildings, possibly located in a city in Italy. They might have been quite striking (in the 1980s) if not for the abhorrent baby blue, pink, and green hues, bordered in age-faded, off-white, wooden frames.

Suddenly, a small figure popped up from behind the reception desk to greet me. I was committed now. My first instinct to duck and run was, unfortunately, out of the question. When I looked at her, my first thought was, how could you have let this happen? The office manager should have understood that this eyesore reflected poorly on the business and its staff. One thing was certain; I did *not* want to work in this mess!

There was an important message that the departing office manager was sending through the disorganization of her surroundings. I discovered later exactly how telling it was about her work habits. She didn't give a darn about the business or the owners. The quality of her work was as messy as her workspace.

I didn't directly blame the business owners. For their sake, I wished they would have recognized the mediocrity that they were enabling and the danger the business faced at the hands of this individual. They were concentrating on their thriving business. The success they were experiencing made their talents apparent. But it all could have been disrupted with a single computer crash and taken months, if not years, to recover. (More later on my discoveries.)

# THE JOB

*"Money isn't everything,
but it's reasonably close to oxygen
on the 'gotta have it' scale."*

## ~ Zig Ziglar

I had few expectations of making a ton of money at a new job. The country was beginning to recover from a crazy recession, and a good job was difficult to find. I was a person who had always had an easy time finding work. With years of experience behind me, I was skilled. Having difficulty finding a job was an entirely new experience for me. My husband and I relocated to Sacramento from Southern California for his work, and I, too, needed to find a job to help with our obligations.

So, there I was, in the office from hell, waiting to interview for a job I knew I was probably overqualified for and most likely wouldn't pay what I was accustomed to making. In that case, I would be selective. If I were not going to make a ton of money, at least I would work at a job that would not be seriously taxing on me mentally. I'd already had my share of stressful responsibilities during my career of forty-plus years. After all, I had visions of retiring sometime in the next few years, and I wanted my last job to be relatively laid-back.

I met with the three business owners, and I liked them immediately. Dave, Dan, and Ken were represented by the DDK acronym that was the name of the HVAC business they owned together in Sacramento. This crazy office was certainly not a reflection of the level of professionalism they portrayed. These guys were pros. Their questions were pointed and professional, and I sensed that we made a connection. I didn't know at the time how successful they had been in their more than ten years in operation.

They had survived the recession that had brutally wiped out so many construction businesses. That in itself was impressive.

The interview went well, and they made me an offer that I couldn't refuse, with the condition that I start immediately. Despite the fact that I really disliked that office, I started working at DDK Mechanical the next day as the new office manager.

It would take me several months to completely remodel that office, but it was at the top of my priorities. It needed to display the professionalism that it currently lacked.

First, I needed to invest in and develop a relationship with the exiting office manager. I would only have access to her for one-on-one training for about a week and a few weekends after that. She made the task pretty difficult with her bad attitude towards DDK. She had tangled with two of the three partners, was bitter, and held a grudge. Her constant bad-mouthing of the three owners was distracting, and I wanted to draw my own conclusions about the guys. I couldn't imagine more unprofessional behavior. I was a new hire, and she owed the owners more respect for employing her for the previous six years. Still, I needed to spend time training with her for the good of my new company. I had accepted the job and was committed.

The office manager and I maintained a connection long after she left me on my own. I spent time making her comfortable with me. She could trust me to listen to her grievances without either judgment or agreement. Because she liked me, I continued to ask her questions by phone and email even years later. How did I do this? (Check out my ten principles in the "Winning Points" section of this chapter.)

# FIND SUCCESS, FREEDOM, AND MAKE MORE MONEY

*"Most people think they give up job security*
*when they teach someone else how to do their job.*
*The truth is, in the right setting,*
*you can have more freedom to learn new skills*
*and pursue other interests.*
*In turn, success might look like a promotion*
*and more money where you are,*
*or in an opportunity elsewhere"*

### ~ Karen Hunsanger

As I began my work, it quickly became evident how vulnerable this business was. The accounting software was old, and the files were corrupted. The system had not been correctly backed up in years. All it would take was one computer crash, and years of records would be lost forever. Once I began digging into the transactions, I discovered reckless entries and the cover-up of lazy work habits going back for years. So much for the easy job I was seeking. This was going to be a challenge. One thing was certain; the office manager had managed her work as poorly as she kept the office. She didn't care!

The situation was dire, but in addition, I was now the only one in the office who knew the payroll and accounting systems. If something happened to me, these guys would be in big trouble. This condition was totally against everything I'd ever believed in, and I needed to correct it. It was essential to build trust with the three owners quickly and get them on board to make critical improvements.

Each of the three was different, but all were champions. Together they had an interesting work dynamic, and their personalities and strengths could not have been more different. They had all left the same company to start a new one. The hierarchy that had been established in their previous environment was still evident. Ken had reported to Dave as an estimator, and Dan was independently responsible for project CAD drawings. They were equals in their new entity, but the level of respect they had in their previous roles carried over.

They had been partners for more than ten years by the time I entered the picture. The business was very successful and well respected in the industry. So, whatever they were doing was working. But it was evident that they didn't have control of their front office, which could have been devastating to their business. Not anymore, however. I was on it!

I began to invest my time in the three partners. Okay, so investing your time into a new boss or client is not an epiphany. Of course, most people will do that. The secret of success, however, lies in your ability to connect. (Look at ways to build trust and form an alliance in the "Winning Points" section of this chapter.)

The partners quickly began to trust in me and my advice. So, when I told them they needed to upgrade the accounting software and recruit their outside IT person to set up a backup system, they understood the value.

Most importantly, they let me remodel that gawd-awful office!

My salary grew substantially over the next five years, and the extras, like merit bonuses, became increasingly generous. I had become one of the most valuable and trusted managers in the company. I developed strong relationships with my three bosses and concentrated on doing the best job I could for them.

At the same time things were beginning to operate correctly in the office, the business was growing. The office work was beginning to become more than a one-person operation. I told the owners that I needed to hire an office assistant, and they trusted and supported me. So, my search began.

Honestly, I failed a few times before I found Brooke. Once she started, though, I knew that the company had found a true asset. Brooke had qualities that set her apart from the previous candidates. First, her personality was fun and engaging, and her attitude positive. She was eager to learn, of course. But more than that, it was important to her to quickly become independent and rely on her capabilities to help others and contribute to the team's overall success. She was driven and determined but not overly assertive. Her work ethic was motivated by producing quality, dependable work, and in her heart, she came from a place of contribution and service. She was a champion worth investing in.

Brooke learned quickly and soon became a valuable right hand. She took so much of the workload off me that I was free to concentrate on other things. This is the *freedom* that comes from investing in someone who can relieve you of your overload.

I was then ready to start thinking about retiring. But though Brooke was a great assistant, she did not have an interest in doing my job. She was satisfied to perform in a support position, and the office needed that. But I needed to find my replacement. Quite frankly, it was stressing me out a little. I had so much difficulty finding Brooke that experience seemed to be a limited commodity. I needed to find a talented person I could train to take my place. I would not leave the partners until that mission was accomplished. I began to wonder if I was going to be eighty before I could retire?

But then there was a fantastic turn of events when the partners decided to expand their business. They would be taking on work that was previously done by a subcontractor. In eliminating part of that contractor's responsibilities, DDK could also take on some of their employees. One of the employees who came to work in our office was Christa. She was already experienced in the industry due to working for that subcontractor. She was intelligent, driven, and knowledgeable. She was my perfect replacement.

# CHRISTA

## EVERY CHAMPION HAS A STORY.

*"You need to find your own way; I don't have the means to care for you."* Her mom's words cut like a knife. Christa was only twelve years old when her parents decided to go their separate ways. The problem was that neither of them had plans to take her with them. Her father never said a word before he turned his back on her and walked out of her life. Her first thought was to cry. But no! She was stronger than that, and instinctively she knew she could figure out how to survive. It was a burden that no twelve-year-old should ever experience.

Her mom didn't offer to make arrangements for her or determine who would care for her minor child. But she promised to send a meager fifty dollars a month to whomever she lived with to help cover expenses. Christa was left on her own to figure out where she would live and how she was going to survive.

She knew that her mom could have been arrested for neglect, but what good would that have done? It wouldn't leave her in a better place. She could have easily given in to the system and been institutionalized or placed in foster care. But she was comfortable in her life. She had close friends and attended a school she liked. While she had the freedom to make her own choices, it better served her character to fight for her future and find a way to stay where she was.

Christa went to live with her best friend, whose mother was already a single mom of four kids. Then, Christa's mother complicated matters by discontinuing the fifty-dollar payments after only a few short months. Her friend's mom was struggling and simply couldn't afford the additional expense after the first year.

Christa then went to live at another friend's house. But that mom was also a single mother and could not afford to let her live there any longer than six months. Christa was still too young to get a work permit, so she continued to bounce from house to house as long as her friends' families would agree to let her stay. At each one, she cleaned and worked hard to try and earn her keep. She did not want to be seen as a freeloader.

Finally old enough to work at fifteen, Christa got her first job at Taco Bell. She was then able to stay with her original friend with an agreement to pay her mom a little money. But she was too young to drive and still depended on her friend's parents for transportation. When she didn't have a ride, she walked for miles to meet her obligations. Sheer tenacity and the unwillingness to be defeated got her through her demanding schedule of work and school.

Then, her life changed forever when, while working one day, she met a boy named Troy. They shared a young love almost from the first moment they met. She was cute and funny and had strength beyond anything he'd ever seen in someone so young. He was sweet and kind and began to help her by buying the things she needed. Troy could see that money was tight for Christa living with her friends. He wanted more for her, and after they'd been together only a few short months, he asked her to move in with him and his family. Troy taught her how to be responsible with her finances, helped her open her first bank account, and made her save her money. He paid for everything from that moment on.

*"You are never going to make it!"* This was the popular chant of the friends who knew Christa when she married Troy and became a mom, all before her eighteenth birthday. They thought she was too young. But she was forced to grow up long before her years should have allowed. That didn't stop the naysayers from warning her that she was throwing away her future.

Today she and Troy have two great kids, Ashley and Jordon. Her kids always came first while she and Troy were raising them. It was critical to her that they understood just how special they were. Her failed childhood experiences never cast a shadow on how she raised them.

Troy and Christa have been happily married for more than twenty years as of this writing. So much for the pessimists— I think she made it just fine!

# EXPERIENCING THE JOY OF INVESTING IN OTHERS

*"Some of the greatest joy I experienced in my career was in witnessing the growth and success of someone I spent time mentoring,"*

### ~ Karen Hunsanger

I was thrilled to have someone with Christa's abilities come to join the DDK team. It was an answer to a prayer. I now had a replacement, a Champion, to train to replace me in my job. That training would allow me to retire with peace of mind, plus I was happy to be helping this young person succeed. The bonus, and the purpose, to begin with, was that I was leaving the partners in capable hands. I spent the next ten months training Christa to do my job. She was so eager, intelligent, and talented that she made the work easy.

Christa will always hold a special place in my heart. I have never met anyone who works harder and takes their responsibilities so seriously. At the same time, her personality, especially her sense of humor, is delightful.

As of this writing, it has been two years since I left Christa in charge of DDK's office. She still calls me now and then. But she no longer needs my help. She has complete control of that office, and I couldn't be prouder of her. What a Champion!

## WINNING POINTS:

The purpose of this chapter is to stress the benefits of mentoring and training others. This can be especially beneficial when it comes to teaching someone your current job. I will admit that the business's climate has to be right for this. There are people and businesses who are cutthroat and are so competitive that the effort can be risky, if not impossible. I hope you will not choose to work with a company in that type of environment.

On the other hand, given the right setting, training your replacement can be personally beneficial, maybe even profitable. Ah, I hear you say. In my story, I was about to retire and, therefore, took no risk in training my replacement. But have you ever been told by a boss, *"I can't promote you to the job you are interested in because I don't have anyone to take your place."* If you have been mentoring an underling, you have a better chance for growth in this scenario.

How many people do you know that are terrified to take time off because there is no one to do their job while they are out? It's a crime. First, I have always believed strongly in cross-training key positions because of the risk to the company when only one person knows a job. There should be a level of commitment to the company team that would never ever allow things to fall apart because of the absence of one person. Second, there is freedom in knowing you can leave your job in good hands when you need to take a well-deserved break.

One final note: To achieve success in cross-training, you must have one important attribute. You must possess a high level of self-confidence when it comes to doing your job. If you are great at what you do and are respected, no amount of training you give others will put you at risk of losing your job. Your employers will recognize your capability and commitment and will never want to lose you. Plus, the other team members will want to learn from you. So be great at what you do!

## LEARNING A NEW JOB — CONNECTING WITH YOUR TRAINER

Investing in people is not always in the role of the teacher. Often, it is the opposite, and the investment benefits you as the student. That self-investment is always worth your time. You must commit to it and give it 100% of your attention and effort.

The following is how I became allies with the office manager I was training with and the ten principles that can help you in a training situation too.

- **Show appreciation** – I let my trainer know that I appreciated her skill, knowledge, and time. How? I acknowledged her expertise, and then I genuinely thanked her for her time. I made it a point to do this often during my time in training.

- **Listen** – Without judgment or the need to always respond. (Enough said.)

- **Find common ground** – I had many things in common with my trainer. For instance, small talk about our mutual love for dogs helped us connect on a personal level. It helped break the ice, offered a distraction and a small break when the training became intense or tiring.

- **Create and communicate goals** – You are the only one who can determine what is likely to come easy to you and what will take more concentration, and you probably have limited time. Write down what you hope to accomplish in the order of priority.

- **Taking action** – It is essential to apply the lessons you are taught in the full view of the teacher. The mentor will quickly lose interest if you fail at this. Do not be afraid to take the reins when they are handed to you. There is a sense of satisfaction a mentor experiences when you "get it." They will want to continue to help you when they see you make an effort.

- **Do not be a "know it all"** – Unless you are a complete newbie, you have a skill level, and everyone already knows this about you. You may even be more knowledgeable than your mentor on specific topics. But it is important to remember that you are there to learn what you don't already know. To make a point or receive clarification on things you may disagree with, ask direct questions. There is no need to show off or constantly challenge your mentor. It is a turn-off.

- **Ask questions and take notes** – It will not only help you with recall at a later date, but you also display a level of interest in what you are being taught. You are showing respect to the mentor.

- **Ask for and accept honest feedback** – Be humble. Be willing to take productive criticism for the sake of learning.

- **Celebrate success** – Give yourself a deserved pat on the back when you make progress. A good mentor will celebrate with you.

- **Keep the door open** – The old line to "not burn bridges" is appropriate here. I had questions that I was able to get answers to until I no longer needed the help.

# BUILD TRUST
# AND FORM AN ALLIANCE
# WITH YOUR BOSS OR CLIENT

Over the years, I have taken notes and made a list of alliance-building actions that have worked for me. I believe they can help you too.

- **Communication:** I know it's a bit cliché and overused as instruction. However, there is nothing more critical to your success and your ability to connect with the others you touch on your journey. Contemplate the four following tips:

1. **Consider different communication styles:** Not everyone communicates in the same way. You need to determine the best way to communicate with the individual you are speaking to. Some people want to hear things in detail, while others prefer to cut to the chase. Some people are very personable and talk on a more emotional level, while others don't like to engage in small talk.

   I am very direct (so I have been told). That style does not work with anyone who is soft-spoken, easily insulted, or might feel my style is confrontational. Have you ever had a conversation with someone who takes a long, thoughtful pause before responding to you? My husband does this, and it used to drive me crazy. However, to successfully communicate with him, I have learned to be patient and let him take his time without interruption. Take the time to learn the communication style of the person with whom you are developing a relationship.

2. **Listen:** Yes, this is as important in communication as speaking is. You cannot possibly learn about the person you are trying to ally with without focused listening. Being present in the conversation lets the speaker know their opinion and input

are valued. You become clear on expectations, and they gain more trust in you and confidence in your abilities. Are you listening?

3. **Repeat:** There is no better way to confirm that you understand an important point or directive than by repeating it back to the speaker. Again, this tactic helps to create trust and confidence.

4. **Follow up:** I am one of those people who will always err on the side of over-communication. Copy pertinent people on informational emails. Jot down notes on a conversation, then share. If what you know can be of value to someone else, share, share, share!

- **Don't take temperament personally:** Unless negativity is directed towards your performance, take a boss's or a client's mood with a grain of salt. Everyone has a bad day once in a while. If they cross a line, of course, call them out. Otherwise, act normally and get on with your day.

- **Demonstrating initiative earns trust:** Don't always wait to be told what to do. Solving a critical problem for the boss or client on your own will earn you huge kudos.

- **Be willing to learn new things:** You aren't always the smartest person in the room. Your boss is your boss for a reason. You can learn something from almost everyone if you open your mind to new ideas.

- **Pick your battles, but don't be an epic brown-noser:** Sometimes, you will disagree. It's okay to voice your opinion respectively. Don't make a habit of constant dissent. But at the same time, don't say you agree if you don't. And for the love of all that matters in the world, do not be a big "yes" person either. It will earn you nothing but disrespect. Plus, it's annoying!

- **Do everything you can to make your boss/client look good:** It's your job, after all, and your efforts will be appreciated, if not rewarded.

- **Be loyal:** *Never* bad-mouth your boss or client to anyone. If you are working with or for someone you don't respect, make plans to move on. Know that you will lose credibility and earn a reputation that will follow you as soon as you begin to say negative things about people.

- **Don't always look for a pat on the back:** Do the job you are being paid for, do it to the best of your ability, and don't expect any special recognition for doing so.

- **Be honest:** Lying to your boss or client will forever taint that relationship. Don't do it!

- **Zero in on the skills that matter the most to your boss/client:** Remember, you want to both do a good job and make your boss/client look good. Understand their expectations and priorities. This point goes back to the importance of communication. Ask questions, and then listen.

## THE RESPONSIBILITIES OF A MENTOR

In Chapter Three, Matt Aitchison gave us some very sound guidance on the responsibilities of a student seeking a mentor. I also wanted to discuss what it means to be a good mentor. Consider the following:

- **Be genuine and committed:** Your student's success depends on your willingness to share your skills, knowledge, and expertise without hesitation.

- **Be patient:** Accept the level of knowledge your student currently has. This is your starting point.

- **Identify the mentees' strengths and weaknesses early on:** Recognize that everyone has areas that could use some work.

- **Encourage and help them to develop problem-solving on their own:** Don't be hasty in providing all of the answers. Ask thought-provoking questions to encourage independent thinking. It increases motivation and confidence. People often learn faster and feel more successful. Remember that you are trying to develop individualism, not a clone.

- **Provide constructive feedback:** Never be demeaning. Instead, be understanding and offer productive solutions.

- **Networking:** Help your student find professional networks and help to open doors for them.

- **Don't have the answer?** If you don't know something, say so. Help to find the answer if you can. A good mentor is also a continuous learner.

- **Communication skills:** Listen carefully first, then ask and advise.

- **Develop mutual trust and respect:** Be honest and follow the above guidelines. Trust and respect will follow.

## EXTRA POINTS:

I want to express sincere appreciation to the three owners of DDK Mechanical for your years of friendship and support during my final journey in the corporate world. You all hold a special place in my heart.

Dave Absher, Dan Goff, and Ken Seastrom

# ENDGAME

It is my true desire that you will decide to crush your challenges and level up to the career or life that you dream of. Don't let obstacles permanently sideline you!

Success is as close as the Champions around you. They can be mentors who are already doing what you want to do and can show you the way. You may find coaches that challenge you or classes and books that inspire and teach you. It could be that your spirituality or God and your faith are your very best Champions. Your Champions might be found in the people you pass the baton to or those you help back up when they fall. Yes, you absolutely get bonus points if you help others during your journey.

I have invested in many Champions throughout my life, and luckily for me, a lot of really great Champions have invested in me. Now, my role has changed, and I am sharing my experience through my writing as an investment in you. I hope you will feel the connection and be inspired to invest in yourself and others too. Your world, and those whom you touch, will become a better place if you do. Reach out and tell me your story at www.karenhunsanger.com.

Remember, *You Are Surrounded by Champions.*

# GRATITUDE FOR MY MVP'S

I owe special thanks to the many Champions who supported me while I wrote this book. You may have thought your input was a small thing, but I assure you that every word of wisdom you offered had special meaning to me, and each of you are appreciated beyond words.

| | |
|---|---|
| Allison Dillard | Alice Sullivan |
| Andy Storch | Angel Hill |
| Anthony Fike | Brigitte Cutshall |
| Charlotte Harrill | Chris Bystriansky |
| Christa Getz | Dani Whitehouse |
| Diego Corzo | Glenda Gardenhire |
| Honorée Corder | Jason Koger |
| Jenny Koger | Jennifer Fike |
| Justin Duncan | Karen Anderson |
| Karen Love | Laura Di Franco |
| Lisa Jack | Marilea Gray |
| Mary O'Donohue | Marie Aitchison |
| Matt Aitchison | Matt Overlund |
| Mike Carney | Melanie Aull Bache |
| Rachel Richards | Ted Hunsanger |
| Terry Stafford | |

# ABOUT THE AUTHOR

## FAN OF CHAMPIONS:

**Karen Hunsanger** is an enthusiastic fan of success stories—especially when the achiever has overcome extraordinary odds. Now retired, Karen spent her lengthy career in both the corporate world and as an entrepreneur. She is passionate about using her experience to help others get past the challenges that are keeping them from reaching their dream career and life goals. She loves to hear from readers. Send her an email at karen@karenhunsanger.com.

Made in the USA
Columbia, SC
03 September 2021